Grigs!

A Beauuutiful Life

Bill Grigsby

Sports Publishing L.L.C.
www.sportspublishingllc.com

Director of production: Susan M. Moyer
Acquisitions editor: Bob Snodgrass
Project manager: Jim Henehan
Dust jacket design: Kenneth J. O'Brien
Developmental editor: Kipp Wilfong
Copy editor: Cynthia L. McNew
Photo editor: Erin Linden-Levy

All photos courtesy of Bill Grigsby

ISBN: 1-58261-717-1

Printed in the United States of America

Sports Publishing L.L.C.
www.sportspublishingllc.com

To my family

Contents

Preface . . . . **vi**

Chapter 1
Childhood **1**

Chapter 2
The Air Corps **23**

Chapter 3
Back to Joplin **37**

Chapter 4
Goin' to Kansas City... . . . .**53**

Chapter 5
Wrestling **71**

Chapter 6
The A's **85**

Chapter 7
Schlitz **105**

Chapter 8
The Scouts **119**

Chapter 9
The Chiefs' Early Years **127**

Chapter 10
The Chiefs' Losing Years **153**

Chapter 11
The Peterson Era **169**

Chapter 12
The Sports Show 177

Chapter 13
The Family 187

Chapter 14
Toastmaster 191

Chapter 15
The Unforgettables 203

Chapter 16
Contributions 219

Preface

I had lived through the Depression and World War II, a life of give and take. Hell, I'm immortal. I've got the world on a string and the string's around my finger. Or so I thought! Then came a sweaty, clammy, wheezy day in mid-October 2003 and a trip to the hospital with my wife at the wheel.

I really do not totally recall the events of the next 18 days.

Oh, I was coherent enough to remember my name on the ninth-floor charts—SULLIVIAN.

Let's see, there was Silky Sullivan, the come-from-behind thoroughbred of the sixties; Bishop Sullivan; John Sullivan, my friend the banker; and John L. Sullivan, the first heavyweight champion. There were other good Irish Sullivans, but I'm afraid the effects of the anesthesiologist's fine work befuddled my already weary brain. I learned later the Sullivan tag was laid on me by an alert hospital veteran who had been through the celebrity wars before and knew the power grid failures that come with.

"And how is Mr. Grigsby today?"

My wife and daughter made the wise decision to tell the press that they would provide updates, thus relieving the hospital, doctors, nurses and other interested parties the burden of battlefield updates. After looking at the strong and steady hands of my surgeon—and in my day I have studied the hands of some of pro football's best—I gave the go-ahead with one request. When I awoke from this ordeal I wanted to see my loving wife, Fran, at the end of the bed. I got not only that wish, but all of our children—Jim, Paul, Ann, Jane and Bill—were at her side.

I was told later that I sang my way into the operating room, one of my jazz favorites that Rusty belts out at the Phoenix—"*hey, bob a re bop*"—and the nursing traveling party came up with the echo verse.

It was new and different, but I was out of it, not a care in the world and with faith in the strong hands of the cardiac team. All of my grown life I have been around professionals—football, base-ball, golf, and roundball—so it came as no surprise that there are pros in green and white. Tenderly but firmly this team of pros slowly brought me back to the real world. I learned from all of them the lesson of patience, and believe me, my patience was sore-ly tested by day eighteen. You see, I lived a life of doing, of get-ting things in motion, of action.

And sitting and lying in bed and walking the halls of the hos-pital were not my cup of tea. I had my share of visitors—Fran and daughter Ann and the other kids until they had to travel off to their lives.

Dennis Watley, Ollie Gates, Father Martin and Fr. Waris, Jim Watson, David Ward and Carl Peterson visited. Some were legal, some snuck in, but all were there to lend support to a guy who one week before thought he was immortal. And you know what? In this case I was.

I was given a program upon leaving the hospital, telling me the various activities I could engage in during the coming days. Week one, I was told, I could walk through my shop—look over my tools. Heck, I never had a shop.

Week two, I could do light things around the house, like mak-ing my bed, but please, no stripping it. Me, make a bed? Week three, resume sex. Are you kidding?

By this time there was a nice nurse lady who came by the house to take my vital signs and encourage me to loftier goals. Week five I could drive myself to the cardiac rehab class—still no sex, mind you, just treadmills, cycles, light weight lifting and watching with excitement the recovering strength and energy as I reached out for a new and strong life.

Through it all I got encouragement from Len Dawson, Watley, and my first broadcasting partner, Merle Harmon. You see, they all are members of the same club—not G men but Z men.

First I got the lesson in patience, then the lesson in discipline. The White Rat (Whitey Herzog), another club member, called with support, as did Buddy Blattner and Lamar and Norma Hunt, even though Lamar was just recovering from his own surgery.

Supporters included Colonel, now Brigadier General, Doug Raaberg and 500 airmen from Whiteman; Phyllis and Hank Stram; my buddy Gary Coleman, head of the network; and a thousand other friends and the gang at the CHOPPER stores.

I was loved.

But maybe the sagest message of all came from my grand-daughter, Sarah, who told her mom on the eve of the operation, "Papa's not going to die yet. There's something he needs to learn. He has unfinished business."

CHAPTER 1

Childhood

The first time I heard a sports broadcaster, I knew that was what I really wanted to do in life. It was just that kind of moment.

Old man Crosswhite lived on the north side of us. I call him an old man, but I am sure that he probably was somewhere in his 30s. But when you are just a kid, everybody over 20 seems to be old.

I would go over to Mr. Crosswhite's house because he had one of those crystal sets with the headset. He would put it on his head, but he would let me listen on the other side of the earpiece. Can you imagine what kind of sway that had on skinny, eight-year-old child of the Depression?

And in the late 1920s, when I was a little kid, the broadcasting of radio sports was just coming into its glory. I got to witness the development of the medium and the early sports broadcasters firsthand.

And you know what? I would have to say that the broadcasters of those days were better than those of today because they offered the total feel and emotion of what was happening. Truly, they were the eyes, ears and sense of the action. They had to lay it out so people could see exactly in their mind's eye what was happening. That is why I have always believed that radio is the greatest medium. It required broadcasters to create a more vivid picture.

On the radio you can tell stories—and sometimes really embellish them—and make the action *really* exciting.

Me doing what I do best.

There were Graham McNamee, Bill Stern and Clem McCarthy. Don Dunphy would do the fights from Madison Square Garden. They were the ones I heard first in my childhood.

McNamee and Stern were the voices of football; Stern had a dramatic delivery, but he sometimes missed plays. Stern would cover his mistakes with laterals and fumbles, figuring, I suppose, that the listener could not see what exactly had happened. McNamee had the classic delivery of a high-paid preacher.

McCarthy and Dunphy would wring out your emotions with their blow-by-blow accounts. Especially exciting was Clem's call of the Kentucky Derby stretch run. Once McCarthy called the wrong winner at Churchill Downs and was reminded of it later by Stem from the dais at a sports dinner in New York.

"You're right, Bill," Clem responded, "but it's mighty difficult to lateral a horse!"

Even then, when I was eight or nine, I knew that was what I wanted to do with my life. It was fun, certainly, but I felt very strongly about it; it was just a matter of kindling and keeping that fire going. When you are little, if you have a healthy spirit and you have a dream like I did, you believe that it can be done. Even though I was pessimistic in my early years because of the Depression and economic hardship, I gradually began to believe that it could be done. I started to think nothing was impossible; after all, what does a little kid know about the realities of life? That outlook has gotten me through my entire life.

My father, Harry Ludwell Grigsby, was a geologist, and there was not much going on in that profession for him during the Depression. He could not get a job, and my mother, Eleanor Amelia Grigsby, was left to keep the family together. I do not know how she did it. Maybe it was part of their heritage. My father was of Scottish-English blood and my mother was German. Mother was born in Connecticut and Dad in Circleville, Ohio.

I was the youngest of three brothers. The oldest, Lloyd, was 12 years older than me, and Jim eight. Because of the age difference between us, Lloyd and Jim were closer, and I was just the little pest, a tagalong sometimes.

As little brothers always do, I looked up to my older brothers growing up. When we lived in Overland Park, Lloyd went to school at Shawnee Mission. That's when Shawnee Mission was just one school in one building. One of his best school buddies was a kid named Paul Miner. Both were on the debate team and became good friends. Lloyd had great speaking abilities, and maybe some of that rubbed off on me.

Later, when Lloyd graduated, he wanted to go to the University of Kansas. And since my dad did not have a job, there was nothing to keep us all from moving to Lawrence.

We moved when I was in the third grade. If you look at my class picture, you would have no trouble picking me out of the 32 kids in the picture. I am the skinny one in the back row in bib overalls. All you have to do is look for the big ears. And big smile.

We lived at 1505 Rhode Island, where we rented a house for something like $25 a month. It was an important move for me, as it had a major impact on the way my life turned out—old man Crosswhite, with his crystal set, lived right next door.

Rabbit Weller lived just up the street. He was a Native American, a Jim Thorpe type. He played for Haskell Institute and was a great running back. At that time, Haskell played all the big schools like Notre Dame, Army and, of course, Kansas. It wasn't considered a junior college like it is today.

Even though I was just a little kid, Weller and I had more than just a casual acquaintance. I would go over there and play with the Indian kids. I still have the scar on my leg from one of our games. There was a brick walk and I ran into it and split open my leg. I will always remember it, solely because it was in Rabbit Weller's front yard.

I was amazed by his ability.

A few years ago, Haskell Institute played a night game at Memorial Stadium at KU, and it was the first night game in 66 years and the first one since Haskell and Kansas played. That was the year that Haskell beat KU 6-0, when Rabbit Weller beat them with the game's only touchdown. The Haskell line probably outweighed by the Kansas line by 30 pounds per man. But they were so quick and the team had absolutely great athletes.

I remember going to that game with a good friend of mine, Jimmy Mott. Jimmy's father was a popular doctor in Lawrence and also the University of Kansas team doctor. And although my family didn't have enough money for me to go to the games, Dr. Mott would take his son, and Jimmy wanted me to go along.

Jimmy and I were constantly together during this time, playing and doing all the things that nine-year-olds do; creating mischief, no doubt. Even though his father was a doctor and his family was pretty well off, comparatively, Jimmy had to sell magazines. His dad felt it was important that he sell *The Saturday Evening Post* door to door. I would have liked to have done it, too, but I could not get even that opportunity.

So Jimmy earned a little extra money from selling magazines, but since he wanted to play rather than go door to door, we took half the magazines he was supposed to sell and buried them in the vacant lot across from my house. I have often wondered what happened when they developed that lot. They probably believed there had been a publishing company on that spot.

Jimmy and I would go to the football games and sit inside the stadium. Because of the hard times, most people had to sit outside on the hill right below the Campanile because few could afford a ticket. Then after the games, Jimmy and I got to go into the locker room. Can you imagine what that was like for a nine-year-old kid? Talk about hero worship!

That also was about the time Glenn Cunningham was running for Kansas, so I got to see him run thanks to Jimmy and his dad. It was quite a story back in the early 1930s. Cunningham had just recovered from serious burns to his legs. He had become one of the premier distance runners of that era.

I was exposed to the greatness of Kansas athletics; even K-State was pretty good back then. And all the while I continued to listen to the sports broadcasts on Mr. Crosswhite's crystal set next door. Between that and watching athletes at KU, I started to develop intense interest in becoming the eyes and the voice of sports.

When I couldn't actually listen to Mr. Crosswhite's crystal set, I would make up games and pretend to broadcast them. I was eight or nine at the time, and my parents would hear me doing that off by myself in my room and could not figure out what was wrong with me.

Meanwhile, my brother Lloyd was getting deeply involved in the university. At KU, he belonged to a house called the "Cosmopolitan House," a kind of fraternity where a lot of foreign students also resided. Lloyd still lived with us at home, but he would often go to the Cosmopolitan House. It housed people from all over: India, China and other areas of Asia.

He had a lot of buddies in the house, especially one from India. Kindakura fascinated me. He taught Lloyd breath control in the process of becoming a strongman, or what they call a weight lifter today. India used to have a lot of strongmen. Kindakura taught Lloyd that breath control was as important as muscle power. He would lay an 80-pound rock on Lloyd's chest and break it with a sledgehammer.

And, boy, was Lloyd's neck strong. There was one time when he took a 125-pound woman, stood on two boxes and swung her with a rope around his neck. Who wouldn't look up to an older brother like that?

Lloyd also learned jujitsu from the Japanese students at the house. During World War II, Lloyd taught it to the Missouri Highway Patrol and later to U.S. soldiers.

Lloyd's high school friend Paul was also attending KU and living with us at our house. Paul, who would later become the president of *The Kansas City Star*, arrived at our house with a check for $100 made out to my mother for a year's room and board. To this day, I still have a letter from my mother that reads: "To Whom It May Concern, Paul Miner has given me $100 in advance of room and board 1931, and if anything happens to me I want this honored."

And like all of us in the family, Paul ate the same potato soup we inhaled every night. In fact, it probably was Paul's check that kept us eating a lot of nights.

Having been born in 1922 in Wellsville, Kansas, I grew up in an era when times were extremely tough. Your diet has a lot to do with your growing process, and that's why today so many athletes are bigger, stronger and faster than ever before. Diets and diet supplements are a science today. That was not the case in Kansas during the Depression.

I certainly knew that because I was so skinny I was not cut out to be an athlete, even though I really liked to play sports.

I was always a skinny little kid. Not only that, but I was very shy. All you could really see of me were two ears; my head looked like a trophy with two big handles. I had absolutely no body.

I always worried that I had something wrong with me. On the days they were doing the tuberculosis tests at grade school I would not go. I was afraid I had TB and it would show up on the test results. The truth is that I was fearful that I would not live too long. It took a long time for me to believe otherwise.

Even by the time I went into the air corps years later, I was still feeling that to some degree. After all, I was six foot one and only weighed 116 pounds. Because of my physical stature, I didn't think I would even get into the service because I wouldn't pass the physical.

But I did. They told me there was nothing wrong with me, and in fact, they claimed that if I turned sideways the enemy wouldn't even see me. Some consolation, eh?

I was used to living in a lot of places by the time I went off to the service in World War II. My family lived in Wellsville only about six months after I was born. But what is interesting is that during the 1990s the Wellsville folks asked me to be the grand marshall of the Wellsville Day Parade. I think it was two blocks long, but I considered it a big honor and still do to this day.

While I was there for the parade, I had an opportunity to visit the little house where I had been born. It was still around, much to my amazement. There wasn't much to it. But I always like to return to the houses where I lived at one time. I love to look through the windows and envision my family in there, my dad, mom, brothers and me. You do that to see yourself in a happy and wonderful childhood.

I did that in Wellsville, but I didn't necessarily see the picture I wanted or I had hoped to see. I do a lot of thinking about those past days, and how my family might have been if it could have had some of the benefits I have had over the course of my life. They did not have the benefits, and since then, I have had a chance to enjoy all the material comforts. Thinking about my childhood and my family is one of the few things that brings me back down to earth. It makes me pretty sober at times.

My family didn't have the opportunity to travel or to see the world that I have been fortunate to see. My mom and dad did not have the opportunity to do the things I have been able to do. I am often disheartened to know that they never got to the point where there wasn't a constant worry about finances. The strongest memory of my mom and dad as I was growing up is their constant fight for survival in the Depression.

Before we moved to Lawrence, we lived in the Kansas City area in Johnson County, across from what is now the Milburn Golf Club. Dad, when he had a job with the City Service Company, was a member of Milburn and played golf.

I have often been asked about some of my earliest recollections. I recall the golf and my mother standing on the bed screaming while dad chased a terrified mouse around the room with a niblick. A niblick is what they called a golf club back in the 20s.

Although I don't recall all the details, I have also been told we had a most protective dog named Beck. Beck would frequently grab me by the rear end of my diaper and pull me out of the street, although there were not all that many cars in those days.

Despite the difficult times, my uncle George, Dad's brother, was fortunate to have a sporty coupe for a while. I got to ride in the rumble seat of that car once. It was only that one time, but believe me, you only have to ride in a rumble seat once in your life at age eight to remember it for a lifetime.

Uncle George later lost that car in the stock market crash and ended up sleeping on a few park benches after that. But like my parents, Uncle George never gave up on life. (Later, when things smoothed out, it was Uncle George who bought me my first legal drink of hard liquor. It was a memorable moment for me in Kansas City's Union Station, when I returned home from World War II.)

I also recall a basement full of gunnysacks with frogs in them and a hundred or so bottles of fermenting home brew. The gunnysacks were kept moist so the frogs would remain alive. Mother would later baste all the frog legs with the home brew and cook them. Even after the repeal of prohibition in 1932, she still did it.

I remember the time when we were living in a rental place in south Kansas City and Dad would walk all the way downtown and then walk home 40 blocks empty-handed with nothing to eat. He would leave the house in the morning in search of a job and just could not get one. All he was trying to do was raise five dollars or anything he could get so mother could make potato or bean soup for the family.

I greatly wish things could have been different for my mother. She had terrible nightmares because of what we were going through. When you always have to worry about things, it eventually takes its toll, and it did on all of us, especially my mother.

She and I would hide when the gas man or the electricity company representative would come to the door. We would hide behind the furniture because we were afraid they were going to turn it off. We knew if they got in the house, that was it.

At night, I would hear my mother screaming in her sleep. It was devastating and it upset me considerably as a little kid. I was not smart enough or old enough to talk to her about it.

Like so many families then, we also were a proud family. And we were not alone. Twenty percent of the United States was out of work. I remember one apartment house we lived in where there was one guy with a job. He lived in 302 and he was the only one in the entire place with a job.

In an apartment building the smell of cooking food has a way of infiltrating the whole building. I cannot forget how great it was to walk into that apartment and smell food cooking. It is a wonder all of us didn't gather around that guy's place. It was that tough. Very tough.

Every once in a while, someone would pop corn and send a dish out to each of the other apartments. It was not very much, but it helped you through the long nights.

Even though it was a most difficult time for us, there were still times that brought smiles and moments of joy for the Grigsby family.

We moved from Lawrence back to Kansas City as soon as my brother Jim graduated from high school. Lloyd, who was one year short of graduating from KU, also moved back with us. He and my Uncle George did landscaping around town while Jim got a job as a chauffeur for the city manager, a Pendergast crony. I went off to Rollins School, an elementary school at 40th and Main.

At Rollins, I learned woodworking and manual training once a week. I remember the guy who ran the department only had one arm, so I never really thought much of woodworking. I could not fix anything anyway, and I still can't.

Again, things got tough for us back in Kansas City. There was yet another time when my father walked to town looking for work and his ears froze. When he got back, somebody told him to put oil on them, which he did. My God, it was awful the way his ears became swollen. I would see this kind of stuff, and it was terribly upsetting.

We moved around so much, it is hard to keep the chronology of my life straight. In my first 12 years, I attended 16 different schools. That sounds disruptive, which it was, but that is probably the thing that made me as gregarious as I became. I had to meet and befriend people very quickly. If I met them the first day of school, I might not ever see them again. I had to hurry up and make friends. And who had time for enemies?

I had the support of my immediate family, and I had a caring extended family as well. Besides my Uncle George, who always remained supportive, there also was my Aunt Ann. She was my mother's sister, and her husband had died young. She always saw to it that at Christmas time we got a box of something, even though it might just be socks or underwear.

She, my Uncle George and my grandfather lived in Joplin, Missouri, and during the middle 1930s we moved there to live with Uncle George. It was a matter of survival, and in Joplin we got to eat. But Uncle George, bless his heart, had children, too, and it was hard for all of us to live under one roof. It was very demeaning and heartbreaking for my family to have to endure that.

George's oldest son would sometimes write on the bathroom mirror, "Why do you have to stay with us? Why don't you leave?" Of course, that kind of thing was especially hard on my mother.

There was another kid, Fred Rheinmiller, whom I played with at that time. Our escape was to play make-believe sports broadcasting. We would do games at one of our houses, and eventually we had baseball and football leagues. We would take turns being the commissioner, creating schedules and broadcasting these make-believe games.

Today, kids have toys, or soccer teams, or many other kinds of diversions. We didn't have any games. Now fathers routinely go to Little League games or soccer games or the many activities that parents and youngsters find themselves involved in. I wish that I could have spent more time with my dad. I regret it very much even to this day that I was not able to do that. In those days, if you played sandlot baseball or football games, you played on your own. Dads were never there. You had a vacant lot someplace and you had a baseball you had to tape because you had already knocked the cover off it.

We didn't have anything but what we could create ourselves. There was no money to buy anything to play with. My main toy was a deck of cards. You can do a lot of things with a deck of cards. I would make up sports games with these cards. I would have prizefights with the cards, football and baseball games. I would sit there and broadcast the whole darn thing with a simple deck of cards.

This, as I look back on it, was an escape for me. I wanted to hide from the real world. That real world was terrible. It was a world of Mother's nightmares, Dad being out of work, bill collectors and the electric company trying to turn off our power. Is it any wonder I began to live in this world of fantasy, sports broadcasting with a deck of playing cards?

Actually, we were not in Joplin long before Dad got a job in New Mexico. He was hired to run a tungsten mine. So we packed up once again and moved on—this time to Taos, New Mexico.

But just as we got settled in New Mexico and unpacked, the mine went belly-up. We turned right around and came back to Missouri, where Dad then got a job running a brewery in Marionville. It produced Mule Beer. It was called "The Beer With a Kick In It."

I don't recall much about Marionville except for one time at a little social at the town church where we were having a pie supper. I had raked a bunch of leaves and made some money for myself, something like 35 cents that I could use to buy this girl's pie. I did not care much about the pie, but I really had a crush on the girl. Thirty-five cents was lot of money back then to bid on a pie, believe me. But some other guy ended up with my girlfriend, and I ended up with a pie made by an 80-year-old woman. The pie, as it turned out, was a mincemeat pie. I haven't eaten a piece of mincemeat pie since.

We actually lived in a pretty nice house in Marionville because Dad did well at the brewery. Of course, we were renting the house. But as so often happened, this was a short period of happiness for our family. The president of the brewery corporation ran off with all the money and left my dad holding the bag. Once again we were sitting out in left field in the mid-1930s.

It was another devastating time for mother, maybe the worst of bad times. She had family heirlooms she had collected through the years that she had to leave behind. We owed two or three months' back rent and the people who owned the house would not let her go back in and get her possessions. She lost things like photos and other family treasures. We had to leave them, and it left a big hole in her heart. It was so heartbreaking for a little kid to see that happen to his mother. It was a terrible thing, and I never, ever forgave those people for it.

From there, again beaten down, we moved back to Joplin and in with Uncle George. When we got back, my dad went to work for Eagle Pitcher, a mining company. It was lucky that he was able to work for them. He handled their land-leasing program.

By this time I was entering Joplin High School and got involved in ROTC, but what I was really interested in was the make-believe play-by-play of sports. I had started that back in Lawrence and was still doing it in high school.

By my junior year I had become interested in speech and oratory, thinking maybe that was more my calling than being an athlete. I just didn't have the physical stature for sports. I was in several plays and also won the Missouri State Oratory Championship in Bolivar. I spoke about the importance of outlawing weapons of mass destruction—poison gas and chemical weapons—in world wars.

At the time, war clouds were again beginning to gather over Europe. I'd learned about the use of poison gas during World War I. I had become fascinated with that subject and had become quite passionate about it not happening again should a war break out. Even today, I'm not interested in speaking unless I have a strong belief in what I'm talking about. I guess that's why a lot of politicians have asked me to introduce them at gatherings. (Come to think of it, I've probably made a lot of them sound better than they actually were!)

Winning the state oratory championship was exciting and made my parents extremely proud. Up until then I hadn't won anything except maybe a couple of pool games.

By the time my senior year rolled around in 1939 I had gotten a job as an usher and later became the house manager at the local movie theater, the Electric Theatre. The marquee read "Where the Hits are the Habit."

I was in charge of showing people to their seats, cleaning up the vomit, making sure there was enough toilet tissue in the stalls, scraping gum off the bottom of seats, then spraying bug killer through the seat holes so the place didn't sound like a wild kingdom when the lights were turned off. I also fetched Cokes for the pretty box office girl and mass-deodorized 500 people on Thursday nights.

I liked the deodorizing part of my job because it gave me a feeling of power. Here I was, just a kid, flit-gunning essence of blossom dust through a giant fan blade into an auditorium full of foul-smelling people. They got the odor, a newsreel, cartoon and a double feature for a measly 16 cents.

I was making something like 25 cents an hour. It was also a time when you could buy a pint of whiskey for 39 cents, and every projectionist we employed had a drinking problem.

The first lie I ever told to a mass audience, in fact, came as a result of one projectionist named Bud we had working at the theater. One Sunday afternoon we were showing Bette Davis in *Dark Victory*. Just about the time when Bud was supposed to change the reels, he somehow began playing a Looney Tunes cartoon. People didn't know what the heck was going on. Then I remembered I had not checked Bud's pockets when he had come to work.

When I got upstairs, he had the reel of film all over the floor, but worst yet, he had a cigarette in his mouth. In those days, film was very, very volatile. If he had dropped the cigarette, the whole place would have burst into flames and we would all have died.

Obviously, Bud had been drinking. I really had to do some smooth talking to him while I reached over, got his cigarette and threw it out the window.

After I defused that situation, I went down on the stage to talk to the audience. "Ladies and gentlemen, the projectionist has suffered a heart attack. If you would like your money back, we'll give it to you."

No one ever knew the truth.

It was also while I was an usher that I learned how to pitch horseshoes. Another one of our projectionists often competed in the world championships of horseshoe pitching. He taught me the secrets, and since it was in my upbringing to learn all games where you were in control of your own destiny, I listened and learned intently. As a result I got to be pretty good at pitching horseshoes.

Eventually I would keep a record of every shoe that I threw. I was, at one point, throwing 500 shoes a day. Eventually I had a 68 percent ringer success rate.

I learned a lesson at an early age, during the hard-luck days of the Depression: The big animals eat the little animals. You had to hone the skills that gave you an individual advantage.

I got a good education, but I learned more about human nature in pool halls and Wilder's Buffet in Joplin than I did in the classroom. It was there I learned how the trained hand and mind have the upper hand when it comes to relieving another person of his money. Joplin was a mecca for pool hustlers, bootleggers and every guy with a con. I was fascinated by the mind games of the hustlers.

"Throwing Off" was the favorite tool used against the stranger in town. The better players would let the chump win a few, then ante up for the kill. I watched how every player took a pool cue off the rack. You could tell how good a player was by the way he held the cue stick. I learned from the pros and paid for my lessons in the quarters I would lose to them.

I also learned that there is always somebody out there who is better than you, so learn how to let them believe that and use it against them.

My most accomplished work on a pool table came years after I had left Joplin in a 20-game match with Willie Masconi, at the time the best in the world. I won six of the games, no small feat. It irritated him to no end.

The skills I developed on the table I used later in my days on the golf course. The cue and putter have much in common. It carried over into bowling, and I eventually had a 220 average.

One day I bested a guy in golf. He then suggested bowling, which I took him up on. By the third day his frustration had grown while losing money to me, at which time he suggested horseshoes. My lessons from the projectionist at the Joplin theater served me well when I won money for a third straight day.

The theater was about three blocks from Wilder's Buffet, where all the bootleggers from Oklahoma, Arkansas and Kansas would go. If you went upstairs you found a bookie joint and the guy who ran it, Paul Summers. Paul knew I was interested in sports and horse racing. So he would let me in the joint, and what an education it turned out to be for me. Paul would not let any other locals in, although there were people from all other parts of the country up there gambling. Summers didn't want to let the locals in, because if they lost and went home without their money, he was going to get busted by the local authorities. Joplin was a hotbed during that period.

In time, I was the one who got to post all the scores of the games people were betting on. There also was a wire service that announced horse races, and I got to reenact that. What a great thrill that was at the time. I really thought I had made it at that point.

I continued to hone my pool table skills and also learned how to hustle a little bit from that bookie joint. Some of the greatest billiard players of the time, like Titanic Thompson, would come in. You should have seen him snooker people out of their money. I picked this stuff up pretty quick. Of course, after a while, I knew all the percentages, all the batting averages and all the important stats in sporting events.

I wasn't such a whiz in the beginning when they took all my money. When I would get home, my mother would ask, "Don't they pay you on that job?"

"No," I would tell her. "It's on-the-job training!"

I would get all that money back later in life based on what I learned there. It taught me human behavior.

Eventually, the top guys in all the games in that room ended up in Las Vegas.

I bumped around a lot between the time I graduated from high school and when I was finally drafted into the service. Although I may not have understood it fully at the time, my life began to gradually become more positive during that time. I guess I had learned enough in the pool halls, bookie joints and movie houses to apply some spin on life.

I needed to make more money and got a job at the Jayhawk Ordnance Plant. I started in the mail room. I got something like $25 a week, so it was quite an upgrade from being theater usher or even the house manager.

But it wasn't long before I was trying to improve my position there, too. I had heard there might be an opening as a cost accountant on all the plumbing and steamfitting supplies. Keep in mind this was a huge ordnance plant at the time of the war. It was an important job, because the plant made a lot of the ammunition and shells for the war effort.

So I went marching right up to the head guy, a man by the name of Alto D. Teel from Birmingham, Alabama. I went up to him and said, "Mr. Teel, I understand there is a job opening in the cost accounting department, and I would like to have *that* job!" Of course, I had absolutely no idea what a cost accountant did.

Mr. Teel thought I looked familiar, like that skinny kid in the mailroom.

"Mr. Teel, I am that skinny kid in the mailroom, but I am ready to lasso all the U-joints, tees and ells so that the war effort will get a good count," I told him flat out. "I guess you were not aware of my background?"

"Frankly, no," he said with a deep Alabama drawl, "but if you have the damn nerve to ask me for the job, I've got enough nerve to give it to you. Furthermore, you will get a $35 dollar pay raise."

The job paid about $65, so things were really taking off for me, it seemed. In 1940, a job that paid $65 a week was like a jump in class in a horse race.

So all of a sudden I was a cost accountant and didn't know a thing about it! That is when I learned I had to use my head and speaking abilities. If you are going to advance in the world you have to be just a little bit innovative and enterprising. Some might call it bull.

Thank goodness there was a bicycle near the office, because I would jump on it and ride it down into the plant complex and sit there with the plumbers, who would talk to me about everything that we had.

I did pretty well, except for the radiators. I really had a hard time charging those darn things out. Later, when I was getting ready to go into the service, I took the entire radiator file and taped it to the top of my drawer in my desk, hiding it. I never could figure out the radiators, and I didn't want anyone to know. I just didn't want to admit failure.

Later, when I was stationed way out in the Aleutian Islands during the service, I got a wire from Mr. Teal asking me where the radiator file was. I told him, and some time later he wrote back saying I was all right for admitting my shortcomings and if I ever needed a job, there would be one waiting for me.

It was around the time I was working at the plant that my brother Jim left for the war. It was something of a blow to the family, because Jim was working for the railway express company and was giving his entire paycheck to mother every week. Lloyd, meanwhile, had gone off to work in Jefferson City with the National Youth Agency. Lloyd was also teaching the highway patrol judo that he had learned back at the Cosmopolitan House in Lawrence.

We were very conscious of the buildup of the war, because Jim was in the air corps and flying B-17s all around the country. I had not enlisted after graduating from high school because I was trying to help out the family financially; it wasn't much, but it was something. The draft was going strong, and as it turned out I was able to pitch in for about two years.

And like everyone of my generation, I recall vividly the morning of December 7, 1941. I was walking out to the Joplin hatchery where two buddies of mine, John Caywood and Bill McManee, and I would play cards together. It was Sunday about noon and someone had a radio on in one of the shops along the way. Suddenly, the program was interrupted with the announcement that the Japanese had attacked Pearl Harbor.

I didn't realize the full impact of that announcement at that moment. I did later on. Caywood would later become a prisoner of war of the German army.

I think everybody assumed at that time we were eventually going to be at war with Germany, but the attack by the Japanese was a blind shot on us. Our government had not indicated to us that it already had information that the Japanese were planning to do something like this. It had been kept under wraps, and that always bothered me. The government knew because of the messages that they had deciphered from the Japanese secret diplomatic codes in 1940. In all we lost 3,457 soldiers, sailors and civilians and property damage was in the millions.

My mother and father had just begun to make it through that terrible depression, and now all their boys would soon be leaving to fight a war. Jim was flying for the air corps, Lloyd had joined the Seabees, and it would not be long before I was off to Alaska.

We had a lot of love in my family when I was growing up, despite the constant hardship and struggle. It was probably the hardest for mother. From about 1929 when the crash hit until Dad finally got a regular job years later, it was extremely hard on her. And then came a time of fear and loneliness because all of her sons went off to the service and war.

What I remember most vividly when the war first began is Mother just sitting there and always worrying. But she knew that I would always write her because I was the one in least danger. She needed to have some comfort in the form of letters. Jim was bombing over Germany and Lloyd was behind enemy lines in Japan. Years later when I returned home, I found my letters and they were bound together, each one of them with a lipstick kiss on it.

After the war, my parents began to find a greater level of comfort in life. Things were beginning to work out for them and my world began enlarging. I found out that the world was brighter than the dark tunnel we had faced; that you could do a lot of things. I started to dream and believe I could do things that maybe a short time earlier I didn't know I could do.

My first foray into sportswriting was as a copy boy at the *Joplin Globe* after I returned from the service. All I know is that I wanted something to do with the excitement of bringing information to people. And, with the ability to do a little talking, I began to see a new future. I saw a chance to turn things around.

Today, as I look back over my life, I believe it worked out very well. I am thankful for the many friends made and opportunities afforded to me through the years.

I am a happy guy, very gregarious, and people know me for that. I have enjoyed what I often describe as a beauuutiful life filled with beauuutiful days. Because of that I am always upbeat.

If I got a gift from my father, it was a sense of humor. He did not have a lot of time to exercise it because his life was always a struggle, but he did have a great sense of humor when life allowed it. When he died, there was no estate or anything like that, but he did leave me his humor, which has carried me my entire life.

But there is another side of me that can cry at the drop of a hat. I can be sitting at home watching something on television and just see somebody whose life falls apart or there is some kind of devastation in their life, and I take it very hard. Those kinds of things bother me greatly. I have to fight those feelings off by simply staying away from wretchedness.

I remember one day I was on the telephone with my daughter and there was a news story on TV about a little girl being pulled out of a well she had fallen into. My daughter finally said to me, "What is wrong with you, Dad?" I couldn't stop crying because they had found her safe.

My wife, Fran, and I can be watching a movie on television and I will say to her, "Does this have an unhappy ending?" If she says yes, then I can't and won't watch it.

In life, I have seen too many unhappy endings.

That attitude, like me, was born during the Depression.

There's a soft fuse in there someplace that goes back to those days when I was a child trapped in a symbolic well. I know I will never get over it.

Growing up in a world of melancholy is scary at times, but eventually you have to take care of yourself. Doing so has given me a strong desire and devotion to overcome adversity, and that has given me a great deal of appreciation for my family and what we have.

My life might not have started out to be so beautiful, but perhaps because I went through what I did with my mother, father and two older brothers, I have a deeper appreciation today of what has turned out to be a beautiful life. I have so much to be thankful for—this beautiful life that God has provided.

CHAPTER 2

The Air Corps

I was such a skinny kid and did not think all that much about girls until I got into the air corps. And then they sent me to Alaska.

The selective service order to report for induction addressed to William Wiemer Grigsby instructed me to report to the YMCA building in Joplin at 6:30 a.m. on October 19, 1942.

There was a small note at the bottom of the induction notice informing me that breakfast would be provided. Also in the fine print was that local board no. 3 of Jasper County would be furnishing transportation to an induction station of the service for which I had been selected.

You were not necessarily drafted into the army. It might be the navy, marines or the air corps, as it was called at that time. You were simply drafted into the service, and to some extent it was a crapshoot where you would go.

Once you were drafted you took tests, and they determined whether you would be in the infantry, artillery, quartermaster, or whatever. I preferred to get into the air corps. I was lucky and my test scores were high. I like to think they were, in fact, in the genius ranking.

Don't get me wrong, though, I am not saying you have to be a genius to be in the air corps. But maybe it helps.

In any case, I was lucky enough to get into the air corps, and then was named leader of a group of draftees on a bus headed to Fort Leavenworth. I am almost embarrassed to say that that was not because of anything that I did in particular but because my dad knew the guy who was head of the draft board. It was a family favor, because my brother Jim had already gone into the air corps.

I had been out of high school about two years before being drafted. The war had not gotten up to full speed by then. Young men did not have a lot of fears about the war. You just did not think about it in those terms. When people were getting drafted and started leaving, no one was getting killed yet. It was simply a matter of building up the armed forces. Back then I remember a popular line, "Goodbye, dear, I'll be home in a year!"

So the expectation was that you would leave for a year and then come home. That soon fell by the wayside. As it turned out, some people did not come back for six or seven years, and thousands never came back at all.

The thought of leaving home was very daunting for me. I had never traveled by myself. I was just a 19-year-old kid who did not have the slightest idea what I would be getting into.

I began my basic training on November 3 at Fort Leavenworth, but they decided they needed me elsewhere and took me out after only a week. Lucky me, I got out of that business of marching at five o'clock in the morning and was put on a train to go to cryptography school in Miami Beach, Florida.

When I got down to Miami I found myself staying in a resort hotel, and I had never dreamed of ever being in a place like that. But it was not winter vacation on the beach. Guards were posted all around the hotel because there was a fear that Germans saboteurs might land on the beaches. You had to be very careful when you tried to get back into the hotel at night. You had to know the correct passwords or how to sneak back in or you might get shot. I was scared I might get killed by one of my own guards. I would come up fairly close to the hotel, watch the guards go around the corner, then run like hell into the lobby.

I was out after dark because the training was held at night, so that was another one of the great benefits during my early time in the air corps. I got to sleep late. All the rest of the guys at the hotel hated me because everybody else had to get up before dawn. Not only that, but I had most of the day to just lie around.

At that point, I kind of felt I might enjoy being in the service. When I was shipped down to Florida it was on a converted train, and remember, I had not been on a train before. So everything was shaping up to be a great adventure and lots of fun.

One day in the hotel we were having a fire drill, and I will never forget one of my buddies, Eddie Boder, was already in the hall when we were filing out. This guy was feeling along the wall. I asked him what the problem was, and he told me he couldn't see where the door was. I realized then that we might be in a bit of trouble if they were taking guys like him. It was that kind of time in the early going.

I remember marching down the streets of Miami singing, "Nothing can stop the army air corps…we used to work in Chicago in a department store…we used to work in Chicago…I used to, but I don't anymore! A woman came in for some cigarettes; I asked her which kind she would adore? Camels she said, hump she got, I did but I don't anymore!"

To this day, I also recall one striking memory of my short time in Miami. When I first got there til the day I left, I remember the smell of fresh oranges in the air. Just walking along, you could just smell it. Everywhere you walked, they were selling oranges from these little stands along the beach to the soldiers.

Unfortunately, the training in Miami only lasted three weeks. One day before they actually told me where I was going to go next I had a strong inkling that it would not be someplace warm when they issued me a parka and a facemask. They needed teletype and cryptography guys up at a big airbase in Great Falls, Montana. There was a ferry base there for Russian-leased airplanes. We were sending Russia supplies out of Montana, and there were also a lot of messages going out of there for the war effort.

And since it was in January, I went from 85-degree weather to temperatures of zero and below.

When I got up there, the master sergeant of supplies gave me my arctic wear and asked me if I would like to visit him at his apartment downtown later that night. He said there was going to be a party. I asked a couple of the other guys about it, and they recommended that I not go. It wasn't hard to figure out why, and I did not take him up on his offer. When I let him know I wasn't interested, he issued me clothing that was at least twice as big as it should have been. I ended up with a parka so big that if the wind caught me just right, I looked like a sailboat going across the ice.

Since I had a top-secret clearance, I stayed in a special barracks with other cryptographers. We stayed on the base but also had an office in downtown Great Falls. It was a group of really great men, highly intelligent and educated.

Our outfit was the AACS—the army airways communications system—that was part of the air corps and had 50 guys in it. I was the kid of the group, and I called everybody else "Pappy." As I think back on it, the oldest member was probably only 35.

It would get as cold as 40 below in Great Falls, but we still considered it a party town, especially when a Chinook wind would come in. It might be 40 below, but in an hour it might go up above freezing if that Chinook wind would blow through town.

All the men were gone from town, so there were a lot of girls available for dances. I wasn't a dancer, but I would pretend to be. The problem was that it wouldn't take long for you to go through all your money. And in Great Falls, everyone was still pretty much living in the wild west days. The silver dollar was king in Montana. The businesses there didn't like to deal in paper money. You would go in a bar with a 20 dollar bill and they would give you change in silver dollars. If you only weigh 116 pounds it doesn't take many silver dollars in your pants to throw you off balance. I had some baggy pants more than once or twice in Great Falls.

We would get paid the first of the month, and I would always end up broke by the fifth and be forced to just lie around the barracks. I was lucky, though, because one of the guys would always loan me five bucks and we'd all be headed to town again. We would go drink beer and chase women. But there was no heavy sex or anything because it was a different ball game back then. When you were in the service back then, one of the first things they did was show you films to try to keep you away from women. They'd scare the hell out of you by implying you were going to catch some horrible disease. A lot of times after you watched those films, you were afraid to look at a girl for about a month and a half.

I was actually working as a code breaker and putting messages into code at this time. But then, out of the blue, new orders came through for me. I was told I was being shipped out to Annette Island, off the coast of Ketchikan, Alaska. I had only been in Great Falls for two months and I was off to a deeper icebox in a C-46, which they affectionately referred to as a "flying coffin." The C-46s were having ignition problems and they were blowing up occasionally.

I had to quickly be in place, so off I went, first to Anchorage and then to Annette. They also had some high-priority supplies on the airplane and there was really no place for me to sit. I ended up having to lie on all the equipment that was also being shipped. Keep in mind it was twin-prop job and it was going to take us between 10 and 12 hours to get there. All I could do was simply lay there, I couldn't go to the toilet or anything.

That is probably the most scared I have ever been in my life, because I knew I was going to die in a damn airplane, the first time I had ever been in a plane. I figured that if I even made it without dying in a crash, I would be eaten by polar bears once I got safely down on the ground.

I didn't die, and I didn't get a chance to pee. Anchorage at that time was even more of a wild west shootout than what I had gotten used to in Great Falls. At that time in 1942, there weren't more than 20,000 people living there. Today there are more than a quarter million people.

We flew into Elmendorf Air Base and I was able to relax, if you can call it that, for five days.

Annette Island had originally been an Indian reservation called Metlakatla. And it was about the same time I went there that the Andrew Sisters had a popular song that went, "Five miles down the road, Massachusetts…" We had our own version, "Five miles down the road, Metlakatla…you can drop your load, Metlakatla…"

The Metlakatla air base was shared by the United States and Great Britain. The Spitfire flyers were sent there to rehabilitate and keep their flying skills sharp so Spitfires and Bollingbrook bombers were stationed there. But unfortunately there were always fights between the Americans and the Brits at the base. Somebody would always get drunk and want to fight.

I was there, though, to do the cryptography, which was funneled out of Metlakatla or Annette Island through the Aleutian Islands.

Every once in a while we would get a three-day pass and take a three-hour crash boat trip over to Ketchikan. It was a seaport for salmon fishing. They had some low-rent sea-faring hotels that we would stay in.

Up until then, my time in the air corps had been more or less an adventure, sometimes most delightful and other times a bit trying. One day, January 5, 1944, however, it would all change and become quite tragic and traumatic.

I happened to be on the teletype machine when a message came in that would change my life. I read it one word at a time, when the message came in that my brother Jimmy had been killed.

It said simply, "The War Department regrets to inform you that Tech Sergeant Jim Grigsby was killed outside Beppo Junction, Utah (sp) when his B-17 went down."

What a shock, and even today it still causes me a lot of pain. The terrible thing about it is that he had flown 50 bombing missions in Europe in 1943 and come back after being shot at constantly. He had been recycled back to the United States to train other pilots, gunners and radiomen. Then to go down in a routine flight was hard to grasp. It made it more difficult for the family because he had survived being shot at over Italy and Germany.

The B-17s had a lot of problems with icing and there just wasn't a good de-icing system. The whole crew, 10 guys, were killed. Jim was the tail gunner and radio operator.

I requested and received an emergency furlough and went home to Joplin to be with my parents when Jim's body was returned. It was very tough flying back. Lloyd couldn't return because he was fighting behind the Japanese lines in China.

It was awful to see the impact it had on my parents. It was a terrible blow to them. We had never had the trauma of someone dying in our family. I couldn't comprehend it as a young person, even though I had had 10 classmates who had already been killed during the war.

They brought Jimmy back by train and the paper there in Joplin made quite a bit out of it. He had been one of the very first airmen to go over to Europe in a B-17. Jim was such a good person and during the hardship days for our family he had worked for the Railway Express Company and had virtually given mother his entire check so we could all eat. He also had a wristwatch that was at the pawnshop half the month. Then when he would get paid he would use the rest of the money to get it back and wear it for the other half of the month. That's the way Jim was. He was 29 when he was killed, and he had planned to be married a few months after the time he went down.

As tough as it was for mother during the Depression, this left her in a serious state of depression. She was already suffering because each of her sons had gone off to war and she had no one at home to fall back on. Dad had finally gotten a steady job and she didn't have a lot of close friends because we had moved around so much.

I spent a week with them in Joplin, and when I did go back to Annette Island I think it was hard on my parents to let me go, although they knew they couldn't do anything about it. It got to them more than it did me because they were still in Joplin with all of the memories of us growing up.

When I went back it was a hectic time because the war was on. The Japanese were making moves on the Aleutians. I was back on Annette only a short time before shipping out to Bristol Bay, Alaska. We had built an airbase there with longer runaways to enable the bigger bombers to land. About the only thing being used out of the Aleutians up until that point were the catalinas and other bombers that were so slow that the Japanese ate us alive. We would get the decoding from the Japanese, who were down at the Kurile Islands where they had their submarine base. We would send 10 bombers down there to drop bombs on a postage stamp. Our guys would have to fly 20 hours, and half the guys would not make it back. They would have to ditch in Russia or maybe go down in Japan.

It was terrible because the flying conditions were just awful. They might have 100-mile-per-hour winds and it was foggy all the time. In the winter, the temperature would fall to 40 below. I look back on those days and wonder how any of us got through it. We had more people leave the service because of Section 8 than anything, which was for mental health reasons. Many just could not handle it, either on Annette Island or the Aleutians.

It wasn't like someone was shooting at you all the time. If there was any shooting it was at Attu, which is at the end of the Aleutian Islands. We would get messages about the number of causalities we had, and most of those were not because our soldiers were getting shot, but because they were getting their legs amputated due to frostbite.

I really had not given my own mortality much thought until one day when I was out walking on the tundra in the early spring. I came across seven crude crosses. I walked over to them and on them were the names of seven women nurses. They had been killed in an airplane crash on their way to serve in the Aleutians.

I think it was at that point that I realized what war and death were. Here were seven young women who had left home at about the same age that I had. But they were buried in a God-forsaken area that no one could ever find or visit.

Seeing that was very depressing, because there was no one with them when they died. I think everyone wants a loved one with him or her when they die so they can have some comfort. I almost cry today when I think about it, and that was 60 years ago.

I was sent to a place called Naknek, which was at the start of the Aleutian Island chain and only about 150 miles from Dutch Harbor where the Japanese had already bombed. We believed the Japanese were going to try to make some inroads into the mainland.

When they went into Shemya and Attu, at the far end of the Aleutians, they had gone in under the cover of fog and we didn't even know they were there. You just couldn't see. When we went in to drive them off, we went into Attu to attack them, but when we got there they had already gone.

Today, and then, that area was a sportsman's paradise. Naknek is just to the northwest of Katmi National Preserve, where some of the best salmon fishing in the world is found. There was a salmon river that was only about 50 yards from my hut. It was renowned, but I didn't fish or care anything about it. When they were spawning you could have walked across the river on their backs. We were always eating salmon. I ate so much that I couldn't eat it today.

A lot of times some of the messages we'd get were ones telling us that there would be generals coming in to Naknek. They wouldn't be coming to talk war strategy or anything like that, but to fish. It always made me so mad, because these generals would fly in to meet an admiral under the pretense of a big conference, but then they would go out to the King Salmon River to fish.

I was at Naknek for about a year and a half. But even though the Japanese were not all that far away, probably the worst enemy we had was the mental strain of being in such an isolated place. The food was terrible, and when we weren't eating salmon, it was Spam. Spam was big. You made Spam meatballs, Spam fettuccini, Spam sandwiches.

Our food was so bad I ended up having a problem with some of my teeth that eventually had to be pulled. That's when I learned about what real pain was all about and how to handle it. We had a Russian dentist, and he would pull teeth without any novocaine or anything. I ended up with three big holes in my mouth. Later they offered me a deal for a partial plate if I would pass up a raise in rank to staff sergeant. I took the partial plate.

It was pretty bad, but we were lucky in one way. There was a bush pilot who would fly whiskey and beer in to us. And remember, people back in the States were having trouble getting it because of rationing. But this pilot would fly it in to us from Anchorage. It was five dollars a bottle for the beer and one hundred dollars for a bottle of booze that would cost five dollars normally.

There were only 100 of us on this base, and after the bush pilot would leave we'd get into the sauce. It definitely was the wild frontier. There was even one island, Ogla-Ogla, where you'd go if you got too bad. We called it Double Ugly. That was an island out in the middle of the Bering Sea between Siberia and the United States. If you got sent out there, you'd have to stay for six months, and everyone dreaded having to go there. Supplies had to be dropped in by parachute.

Later when I talked to other soldiers who had been in battle or in prison camps, they sympathized with us. When you don't see a woman for almost three years, your mind starts playing tricks on you. "Are there really women?" you start wondering. I remember one trip we took after he had heard a rumor that there was, in fact, a woman about 150 miles away living with a trapper, who had been in jail back in the mainland and who had run away to Alaska. So we got a Jeep one day and three of us forged at least three rivers just to see if the rumors were true.

As it turned out, it was true, but she was the worst thing you have ever seen. And the trapper was very protective of her. We went into this little shanty and he brought every one of us to our knees when he shook our hands. He was that strong, but also he was giving us a message, "Stay away from my woman." By the way, their clothing was urine-cured.

I was 21 years old at the time and shortly after that, I was offered a deal that if I would sign up for two more years in the service I would be able to take a 30-day leave for a little rest and recuperation. I went back to Joplin, but whether it was the long trip back or being able to see women again, I ended up with a stomach problem at the army hospital in Camp Crowder in Neosho, Missouri. While I was in the hospital, the Japanese surrendered.

Still, I had already agreed to stay in the service for two more years, so after I got out of the hospital and went back to Joplin for the remainder of my R & R time, I bid all my buddies goodbye. My orders took me to St. Louis, and much to my glee, the orders there said I didn't have to go back to Alaska. Oh, was I happy. The year was 1945.

Instead, I went to the air base at Santa Ana, California. That was culture shock, baby, going out there. I didn't do much at Santa Ana except party a lot. I put on a couple pounds from drinking, but I was still, at age 24, pretty skinny.

During this whole time in the service I still had a lot of interest in sports. One day a bunch of us from the air base went over to the Los Angeles Coliseum, which had been built for the 1932 Olympics, to watch the College of Pacific play USC in football. Pop Warner was the coach of the College of Pacific, which only had a squad of 18 players because so many young men were still in the service. There were 150 Trojans, even during the war. USC won big.

I don't remember much about the game except that I bitched the entire game because of the bad seat I had. Finally, the guy sitting next to me said, "Look, soldier, you got in here free, I had to pay for mine, so stop your complaining." I sat in the last row underneath the clock, and later on when I would broadcast either college or Chiefs games I would always go back there and sit in that same seat that I had sat in decades earlier.

Most of the guys I was in the air corps with are now unfortunately dead. We all became extremely close because we shared the same problems and hardships. Most of the guys never thought they would get back alive.

But most of us did. One guy was a professor at Harvard, and another a newspaper man in Cleveland. One of them, though, I still am friends with today and that's great. He is Jake Karnofsky, who had come from an acting family from Wilkes-Barre, Pennsylvania, and who later changed his name to Jim Karen. He had been on Broadway as a kid and was later in *A Streetcar Named Desire* with Marlon Brando and directed by Elia Kazan. Jake and I had a lot of fun, because I've always been a ham. We first met on Annette Island and went to Naknek together.

I talk to him quite often. He lives out in Hollywood, and his wife Alba also produces movies. He has been quite successful for 50 years in a very tough business. Some of his best known films are *All the President's Men*, *The China Syndrome*, *Poltergeist*, and *Wall Street*. He was also a regular on the sitcom *Eight is Enough* and the cable series *The Larry Sanders Show*.

When he was working Broadway in his earlier days, I would visit him at his apartment. And we still get together whenever I'm out on the west coast for a football game or something. He was in the same acting class as the late George C. Scott and Jason Robards, and the three of them ended up very close friends.

But those air corps days are not ones I remember fondly or talk about much now. It was wartime; a miserable time that I just push aside now. I am not a person who lives in the past. It's just that when you look over your life in total, you have to sift through some of the rubble. At the same time, I acknowledge that serving in World War II in Alaska was not the typical war experience. Today, I love Alaska because it's such a beautiful area.

Eventually, in the later days of my service, a system was devised so you could be discharged if you had earned enough points. And although I had signed up for the additional two years, I found I had earned enough to be discharged. As it turned out I got extra points for having served in the Asian-Pacific Theater.

My rank at the time of separation was Sgt. I received a victory medal, an Asiatic Pacific theater ribbon, good conduct medal, an American Theater ribbon and a total amount of $253.03 from the air corps.

I was still skinny at six foot tall and 132 pounds.

On Thanksgiving Day, 1945, I remember walking across a stage in an auditorium in Santa Ana to get my official discharge. They were playing, *Kiss Me Once, Kiss Me Twice, Kiss Me Once Again...It's Been A Long, Long Time.*

I still feel the fraternity of the air force and have kept close ties. I frequently visit my buddies at the Whiteman Air Force Base near Kansas City. I have even gotten aboard the B2 Stealth Bomber.

CHAPTER 3

Back to Joplin

I couldn't wait to get home to Joplin.

I really wanted to see my folks. Mother was not doing well, and I wanted to get back to see what I could do to help her. I wanted to make her life a little better.

It never entered my mind to stay in Santa Ana or California. The trouble with resort spots like that is that the people who truly enjoy those kinds of places have money. They CAN enjoy it. If you don't have money, you have to so much you can't enjoy it. It's like the guy who buys the house for the spectacular view and then can't enjoy it because he's working all the time to pay for it.

I had been thinking for some time about what I wanted to do once I got out of the service. The government had come up with several programs. One would give you $60 a month to pay for college tuition, which I thought was the direction I wanted to take once I got back. The other was what they called the 52/20 Club, where you got $20 in unemployment for 52 weeks.

But I wanted to get into something where I could make a little money and meet some girls. Remember this was 1946, and I was 24. I had become a grown man but still had not begun college yet. When I got back to Joplin, I went down to the newspaper because I knew a guy there by the name of Ray Cochran who was the managing editor of *The Globe*. I had known him when I had been a copy boy as a kid.

I was told they would have loved to put me on the sports desk, but there was nothing open. Instead they put me on the obits. I hadn't been back very long, and I wanted to go right to work and get going, so I took it. I wanted to get into my life. I thought maybe I wanted to be a newspaperman.

Lloyd, meanwhile, was discharged a short time after I had gotten out. He had gotten married, and he and his wife moved to Jefferson City, Missouri, where she was working. Lloyd had become quite a favorite over in China before he left the Seabees. In fact, for years after the war, the Chinese government in Taiwan invited him back to be honored. He never went back.

I lived at home once I returned. It was shocking. Mother, I realized, was becoming senile. I had been home only a short while, and I had asked her to fix me something to eat. But she couldn't remember how to do it, although she had always been a great cook and always welcomed making me a meal.

On another occasion I brought home some steaks, and when she never got around to cooking them I asked her where they were and she told me, "Oh, they weren't any good, and I had to throw them all away." She couldn't remember how to cook them, so she would hide it by throwing things away. I could see what was happening. Every time a train would blow its whistle or she would hear a bugle blowing, she would start crying.

She never ever got over the war and Jim dying. I really blame it on the hard times we had. Dad was working at Eagle-Pitcher and came out of it fairly well, although it left some deep scars on him as well. By this time they were in their fifties, which seems so young by today's standards.

But I didn't spend as much time at home with them as I should have. All the guys I knew had survived the war, and we were friends. We would go out drinking beer and staying out til two or three in the morning dancing and having fun. We had never done any of that.

You're supposed to be doing that when you're young. But I have since looked back and said to myself, "God, I wish I had stayed home more with my folks. Maybe I could have done something." I was good to them, but I didn't stay home as much as I should have.

Even though I hadn't worked very long, I quit the newspaper. It upset me to think that the guys I had come back with and who were doing nothing were getting $20 a week and I was only getting $18 working 40 hours. Besides, I didn't really like writing about people's deaths.

Instead, I decided I would go to college. It was $60 a month and I chose the University of Missouri-Columbia. That was in the fall of 1946 and a lot of guys coming back from the service were doing the same thing. As a result it created something of a culture shock in the teaching ranks for the colleges. The professors had never been challenged by anyone in their classes. All they had faced till then were kids coming out of high school. Now, all of a sudden, the profs had students who had been killing people during the war or who had nearly been killed themselves. It was hard for college administrators to adjust to this new kind of older and grizzled student.

A buddy of mine, Art Chaves, and I went up to Columbia together. We had a tough time finding a place to stay but finally found a place that was owned by a guy on the athletic staff. It cost us $25 a month for a room upstairs and we moved in on a Friday the day after we arrived.

They didn't give us a key though. Off we went to downtown Columbia to drink some beer. We didn't get back to the house until sometime after midnight. Of course, we couldn't get in so we banged on the door until they let us in. They weren't very happy with us and told us they would appreciate it if we didn't stay out so late.

"Wait a minute," we told them, "We're grown men!"

Even worse, the next day the guy's wife asked us how often we planned on using the bathroom.

"Why?" we responded.

"We entertain a lot and since the living room is between your room and the bathroom, we'd appreciate it if you wouldn't go too often!"

At this point, we hadn't even unpacked all our things, which we were carrying around in our service duffel bags. On Sunday, the landlord stopped us while we were headed to Columbia for breakfast. He was curious why we hadn't unpacked.

"We just got back from the service and we didn't unpack for three years," I explained to him. "And come to think of it, I may not unpack ever while I'm staying here...and I may not even come back today."

We didn't. Both Art and I went back to Joplin after the weekend. Our entire career at MU lasted a mere two days, but we had had a good weekend while in Columbia. We could see that it was going to be a miserable existence. We were just back from the war and wanted to enjoy something of the world.

It wasn't too late to get into Joplin's junior college, which is exactly what we did next. The junior college was a lot like MU and all the colleges around the country; there was a big influx of older students. It was a new challenge for all concerned.

It was about this time I was also halfway thinking about becoming an Episcopal priest. Becoming a priest, I believed, would combine helping people and public speaking.

Remember, though, that the Joplin area was known as the Bible belt. If a person was a Catholic in the Bible belt, he often had difficulty keeping a job.

The Ku Klux Klan was also gaining strength during this time. This bigotry bothered me as I began college, especially since I believed that was why we had fought the war.

In one particular English class, the teacher kept downgrading Catholics. After a while, I would argue with her about it. In order to do that I would visit the rectory and talk to three priests—Art Tighe, Jimmy Lyons and Father McBrien—who would later go to Kansas City and have a big impact on my life.

I got my ammunition from them for my discussions with my college instructor. For two years, I would go up to St. Peter's parish in the evenings, which eventually led me to joining the Catholic Church in 1948.

My boss at radio station WMBH-AM, where I was working part time, told me it was the biggest mistake of my life. But then again he was Brick Poyner, the man who had hired me and told me I probably would never make it in broadcasting. And as far as it being a mistake, it was one of the most important decisions I've ever made because I also met my wife, Fran, in the church.

As for my broadcasting career? Well, I'm now in my seventh decade and still counting.

I also had another instructor by the name of Harry Goekel, a brilliant man who was able to relate to the older students coming back from the war. He and the other ex-GI students would go out to have a beer or two. We later formed a drinking club and would pontificate over the heavy issues of the day over a suds or two.

The drinking club was an unofficial club, but the dean of the college did establish a returning veterans association, of which I was elected president, I'm proud to say. We became quite outspoken and active, especially during one bond election to improve the college.

The Globe, the very newspaper I had worked for, came out with an editorial during the campaign that accused us student veterans of getting involved just to better our grades. They claimed we were supporting the bond issue to butter up our teachers and the school. I called the veterans together for a meeting in the gymnasium. I'll never forget that day.

"Fellas, what are we gonna do?" I asked them. "Do you wanna go down and march together on the Joplin *Globe*?"

They wanted to, but I got them to agree to let me go down first and talk to the editor. All we wanted was a retraction and an apology. I ended up having a meeting with the editor, who was a hardnosed redneck.

"I tell you what, I can't hold these guys back," I told him, "and I don't know what they'll do when they come down here. Anything could happen. I'm just thinking about your safety. I want an apology!"

I had to put a little fear into him because the guys were mad. And God only knows how many people some of these guys had killed during the war. The next day the newspaper came out with an apology. The victory was sweet.

But not as endearing as a young woman who I had met at church and who was also at the college, Frances Genser. I had heard that her boyfriend was out of town and that she was going to be at a school picnic, which I, not so coincidentally, decided to also attend. I had taken a liking to her. She was six years younger, and later we would discover that her mother was very upset by that. On May 10, 1947, which also was her mother's birthday, we met at the school picnic.

Afterwards, a bunch of us were going to head over to the Cotton Club in Joplin, and I asked her to go with me. Somehow she was able to talk her mother out of having to go to her birthday party and off we went. We danced and had a good time.

The next time we went out I asked her to marry me.

It took her three years, but eventually she said yes.

I was also working for a letter shop during this time. We put out bulletins or mailings. Different churches would hire us to put out their newsletters. I learned about editing and the perils of sloppy headline writing.

One day this little minister came running up wide-eyed, saying, "Look what you've done to me!" What I had done was put out a headline that read, "The choir will lead in the sinning."

Despite all these things, I would later in life be honored as the outstanding alumnus of the college. That was about 15 years ago and they had a big day down there for me. There was even a parade in my honor. Can you imagine?

Everybody associates me with sports broadcasting today, but my roots are deep in news and not just as a rip-and-reader. I think I was a pretty fair reporter for WMBH in my early days. In 1948 when Harry Truman was running for re-election against Republican Thomas Dewey I did a man on the street poll that

Fran, Harry and me.

indicated that Truman was going to win the election, which went against the popular thinking at the time.

The boss was a bald-headed, hot-tempered staunch Republican, and he gave me hell for doing the poll and claiming Truman was going to be the winner. He accused me of fixing the results because I was a Democrat and that I was going to make the station a laughingstock because Truman was not going to win. He said to remember that the only people I interviewed were the people on the street.

I kept explaining to him that it had nothing to do with what I was hoping for, but it was a true reflection of what people were telling me. And even though it went against what everyone was saying nationally, the only way of knowing the truth was to wait until the election results came in. But the fact was I would ask people whom they were going to vote for, and every day Truman would win. And remember this was in southern Missouri, which was an enclave of Republican strength. I believed in the poll, and I personally believed, because of what people were telling me on the street, that Truman would win.

I also covered his victory train when it came through Neosho, too. That was quite an event. The train came through at five o'clock in the morning and about 10,000 people showed up to see it. It rolled in about a month before the election.

The Truman campaign went across the country in this train, and every once in a while they would have to stop the train in a city to raise more money in order to keep the train moving. The morning it stopped in Neosho was quite memorable, with the crowd screaming, "Give 'em hell, Harry…Give 'em hell, Harry!"

I even had a chance to meet him and was impressed by what a simple, regular guy he seemed. He was a Missourian through and through. I guess it solidified my Democratic roots, but I never tried to hide the fact that I was a strong Democrat in Republican territory. And I was a strong Democrat not because of my parents' views, but because I felt that the Democrats better represented the interests of the common man. I was a common man and still feel that strongly about it today.

Later I worked very much on behalf of Tom Eggleton and Stuart Symington, but still believe strongly in the work of Republicans like Senator Christopher Bond.

I might also point out that Dewey also came through Joplin during the campaign and I covered that with just as much enthusiasm as Truman. My memory of Dewey is that his whole campaign that day was very calculated. I remember him by the fact that every hair was in place and he was very much a straight arrow; a typical New Yorker and, dare I say, very plastic compared to Truman. I remember at the time thinking that Dewey wasn't going to win anything because of his personality, even though everyone was still convinced he was going to be president.

Covering the campaign trains was a big story for me at the time. But I also had a chance to cover and be involved in another national story that proved even bigger than Truman and Dewey.

It was the infamous William Cook murder case.

I am a lifelong Democrat, but greatly respect Missouri's senior Republican Senator, Kit Bond.

The Carl Mosser family was passing through southern Missouri on vacation from Atwood, Illinois, when they picked up a hitchhiker by the name of Bill Cook. He turned out to be psychotic and held them for days in terror.

People nationwide were aware of their absence and it kept gaining interest as every day passed without them turning up. The whole family, five all together, just simply vanished. Eventually the trail led to Joplin.

There were reports that they had been spotted and they had tried to signal people that they had been kidnapped. Apparently it spooked Cook, because he started killing them until he had killed the whole family, including the family dog.

One day, while I was at the radio station I got an anonymous telephone call from someone (and to this day I don't know who it was) that the Mosser bodies had been thrown down a mine shaft near Joplin. At this point, the search had been going on for about a month, so every tip was being taken seriously.

"You'll find the bodies in the mine shaft on Fourth Street," the caller told me.

Cook was still on the loose, and was believed to be in California by this time.

As soon as I hung up, I immediately jumped into my car and raced to the mine on Fourth Street. Just as I was pulling up, another car was also pulling in. A guy got out and identified himself as being with the FBI office out of Kansas City. We both walked over to the cover on the shaft, moved it aside and sure enough, the bodies were lying in there. The first thing I thought about was to never, ever again pick up a hitchhiker off the road. And I haven't. It was an incredibly gruesome sight that I will never be able to put out of my mind.

As awful as it was, I was a newsman and immediately reported what had happened. I also called the Associated Press, which put out the first bulletin that the bodies had been found. It was an enormous scoop at the time, and I was later highly praised by the wire service for having the presence to stay professional in the wake of such a terrible discovery.

"Our special thanks go to Bill Grigsby of station WMBH of Joplin, Missouri, for his fine coverage this week on developments in the William Cook Killing Case," the wire story read in the 6:30 A.M. regional split.

"Almost instantly after the first tip in the case, Bill Grigsby was in with word...that the bodies had been found. Bill's tip gave us the first publishable bulletin, which let us get a fine beat over the opposition...

"It made a nice six-minute beat for the A.P. Thank you, Bill Grigsby."

Like everybody believed, Cook turned up in California where he had killed several other people, including some fishermen. Cook, when he found out the Mosser bodies had been found, confessed to the FBI and because of my earlier cooperation, I got that scoop, too. I was the first to break the news he had confessed to all the killings.

Today, if you visit the FBI building in Washington, D.C. you'll find a picture of Mad Dog Bill Cook. Once when I was there I got to visit headquarters and meet J. Edgar Hoover. We talked about the case and Mad Dog.

Even though I had been completely involved in the Mad Dog Cook case and the campaign train stories of 1948, my time at WMBH was reasonably routine. Not as routine, say, as writing obits at the *Globe* newspaper, the company that owned the radio station.

I guess that's why I began working at the station in the first place, to cover exciting events. But as anyone who started out in small-town radio knows, you end up doing everything at the station when you're first hired.

I started out doing a farm show at five in the morning, and then did the news thing. It was a cliché, but I'd rip the copy off the wire machine and make a mad dash into the studio to deliver it. I was also selling time, and when they found out that I could broadcast baseball they had me doing that. The station manager asked me one day if I had ever done play by play.

"Sure," I mumbled, not about to explain that it had been in my bedroom as a kid, and the games and players had just been in my imagination.

It was a great thrill when the opportunity to call the Joplin Miners games blossomed before me. The Miners played in the Class C League of the Western Association, and although it wasn't the big leagues, it was as far as I was concerned. Especially since the Miners were also affiliated with the New York Yankees.

The regular announcer, Charlie McIntyre, had been there for 20 years but had hurt his back and couldn't get up the stairs to the press box at Miners park.

Doing those games on the radio was one of the great moments of my life. At various points the Mantles, the Sieburns, the Herzogs and Lumpes would come through the organization. They were men who would later also have a part to play in my adult life. A good part.

I don't remember the first game that I broadcast. It was probably because I was so scared, not because it was my first game, but because the press box sat up on top of this creaky old stadium. The wind would blow and it would sway. And there was no toilet up there, so you had to learn how to regulate your kidneys.

The sportswriter from the *Globe* was also up there in the booth next to me, and he would knock once if it was an error and twice if it was a hit. One day he knocked so hard, he knocked all the pop bottles over in my booth.

I also was under orders not to ever mention weather by the owner of the team, Harry Satterlee. And one night we were having an awful storm—a tornado, hail and rain coming down. I mentioned it on the broadcast and he called me in the next morning.

"I told you never to mention the weather," he scolded me.

"I know, Mr. Satterlee, but lighting almost blew us off the air."

"Don't do it," he said, "because it hurts the crowd."

In my many years in broadcasting there were only two people who ever interfered with my air work. They were Harry and Charlie Finley.

But that's how cheap Satterlee was. If someone would hit a foul ball into the street, the general manager, Roy Beavers, would jump out of his seat and chase it down. He would even go to someone's door to get a ball back. Before games, the umpires were told to take old balls and put white shoe polish on them for night games. Mickey Mantle would get mad at Satterlee because Mick was only allowed six bats.

In 1951, when the Miners won the Western Association by something like 20 games thanks to Mantle, Satterlee was so tight that he wouldn't buy new bats near the end of the season. They eventually got down to only four bats for the entire team. By the time the season ended, Mickey was so mad that he ripped his uniform off and threw it away. Didn't want any reminders, he said.

Jack Fette, who later became a highly reputed National Football League official and representative of the Wilson Sporting Goods Company, also was a young umpire just coming into the league. One Sunday afternoon we were getting ready to play Topeka, the Miners' biggest rival. It had rained hard earlier that morning and the grounds crew was out on the field trying unsuccessfully to get it ready for the game. As it turned out we were expecting the biggest crowd of the year, so Harry went to Jack Fette before the game.

"Jack, we've got to get this game in," Satterlee told him.

"But it's nothing but mud, Mr. Satterlee."

"I don't care, it's dry enough. We've got to get the game in, dammit. I'm in charge of starting the game. If we say start the game, then the umpire starts the game! Understand?"

"Whatever you say, Mr. Satterlee."

So here we go, Joplin against Topeka. Never mind the field is a quagmire. The players take the field, the pitcher warms up and the first batter comes to the plate. The first pitch comes firing right in there.

"STRIKE ONE!" Fette bellows.

A short pause, then he follows up in an equally vociferous tone.

"THE GAME IS OFF!"

Fette had called the game, and Satterlee and Beavers went wild, chasing Fette all over the ballpark and calling the league president, Tom Fairweather.

Of course, Satterlee had to give all the money back to the fans who had packed the park. It was the first time I really got to know Jack Fette, and we've been good friends ever since. Later when I came to Kansas City, I refereed high school and small college football games with Jack, who to this day still lives here.

In the early going of my broadcasts of the Miners, the station couldn't afford to send me on the road with the team. So we re-created the games by using wire copy. Ronald Reagan used to do the same thing when he was a Cubs broadcaster. You have to be a little nuts to be able to do it, so I guess that tells you something about the former president and me.

In the final championship game between Joplin and Topeka, we had to do a re-creation since it was being played in Kansas. With the series tied at three games apiece, I was reporting a pitcher's duel and Topeka was holding a tenuous 1-0 lead in the eighth inning. But the truth I found out later was that Joplin had scored four runs in the second.

What I did was get the Miners those four runs in the top of the ninth. The problem, though, was that the *Globe* reported the big, four-run second inning. Later that day, some guy came up to me and asked if I had been in the sauce the night before. I just told him that damn newspaper would lie about anything!

I had finally convinced Fran—and her mother—that Fran should marry me in 1949. There were six girls in their family, and every time I'd go over to the house I'd announce that whichever one of them was available I would marry. They knew I was kidding. I think.

Even though I was doing the Miners' games and was on the radio, Fran could have cared less. I wasn't Edward R. Murrow or anything. She had a job at a department store. I also had decided to go to the University of Kansas, so I would hitchhike back on the weekends to be with her. I had to quit, though, in 1948, when my mom's health got much worse. I came back and really had to dig in, especially after we were married.

We only have one picture of our wedding. I borrowed my brother's car and $100. We went to Kansas City on our honeymoon. It's sort of a hazy time, because so much was going on in our lives. Not long after we were married, my dad died after an accident at Eagle-Pitcher.

Mom moved in with us in a rented house on the east side of Joplin. It became too difficult because Fran was pregnant, and poor mother was having just an awful time. She eventually had to be moved into a nursing home where she stayed until she died in 1954. Both mother and dad were 66 when they died.

Jimmy was born in 1950, and my second son, Paul, came along about two years later. Paul was born the same day I was broadcasting a Western Association game between the Miners and Muskogee. He and Fran were nice enough to wait until the end of the game before Paul was born.

There was a lot of growing pressure, especially since I was also serving as the commissioner of the Amateur Athletic Union of Southwest Missouri. But I've always lived in a pressure cooker. I felt like a juggler; when you've got a lot of balls in the air, you somehow have to keep track of them. As a result I learned to adapt and shift my focus to a lot of different things.

It was fun doing the baseball games on radio and I loved doing them, but I was only making about $40 a week. And not only was I doing the baseball games, I was also selling time on the broadcasts and was the farm editor at the station. I was never home. And since I wasn't making enough money, I also took the part-time job with Thurston.

I was hired as a farm expert. Fancy that.

I had told them that I'd never been on a farm, so what kind of farm expert did they want me to be?

"Aw, you're a good speaker, we just want you to go into places like Oklahoma and sell fertilizer to the farmers," I was told.

And so off I went spreading the good word—so to speak—of the Thurston Chemical Company. But I didn't just sell fertilizer, I was known as an agronomist, and in some instances, a *noted* agronomist. I have one newspaper from Guthrie, Oklahoma with a headline that reads, "Noted Agronomist in Town"!

Then after I would speak I'd get a copy of the follow-up article quoting people saying they had learned more about farming in that one night than they had in a full year. On one occasion I took 100 farmers and county agents to Chicago to the International Livestock Exposition. Some of the farmers had never been off the farm, much less to a big city. Some of them got so drunk at the hotel, I almost went to jail.

Bill Bowers, who owned the Marco Mills Feed Company in Joplin, came to me one day after hearing me speak.

"Bill, I know you're starving to death with the kids and all," he said. "I can get you a job paying about four times what you're making here in Joplin. You'll have to go to Kansas City if you want to make the change from sports broadcasting to full time in the farm thing."

Well, you can imagine the temptation if you get an offer to make four times your paycheck. I didn't think about radio sports so much as I did Fran and the two boys, Jimmy and Paul, at that point.

During this whole time, though, Fran never, ever second-guessed anything I did. And I was determined that she wouldn't work and would stay home to raise those children. I didn't care how many damn jobs I had to get; she would be there when the kids came home from school.

I quit WMBH and Thurston and bought a train ticket on the Kansas City Southern for $6.25. This was in November, with Fran's birthday just around the corner. I told her she and the boys would join me later in Kansas City.

CHAPTER 4

Goin' to Kansas City...

It probably wouldn't surprise a lot of people that Bill Grigsby's first big job was spreading fertilizer. And as most know, I can spread it on pretty thick, even today. But I am talking spreading fertilizer literally, not figuratively.

Why did I sell fertilizer, one might ask? Simple—survival.

Because I was broadcasting for WMBH in Joplin and wasn't making enough money, I naturally had to consider just about any- and everything for more money. Getting a family started and needing more money, I looked around. And by this time I had developed certain speaking abilities and could present a pretty good case for myself.

I knew two of the executives with the Thurston Chemical Company. They wanted me to do some speaking around the Midwest, especially the farm areas of Oklahoma. At that time after the war there were a lot of agricultural programs going on: Ag groups were sprouting up as the veterans were coming home and getting into the farming business.

There would be ag groups in every little town and every county. They would meet with the county agents and learn farming practices. Oklahoma, in particular, was one big pasture. We were selling a lot of fertilizer to cattle ranchers. Beef was the main commodity.

Thurston would get a lot of requests for a speaker to come out and talk about crop rotation, fertilization and things like that. Ag stuff. The truth was that I really didn't know a lot about this kind of farm stuff, since I had not grown up on a farm. But I know how to talk.

They told me, "Bill, just tell them to use fertilizer and phosphorous and everything will be great." But I also read all of the books, and after about three weeks I emerged as a farm expert.

There might be some who would suggest that it was a great irony that I started out selling bull early, but I don't really look at it that way, because it was a serious business at the time. I was trying to make a living for my family. I wasn't making a lot of money in broadcasting sports, so maybe my career was limited there, and I had a family and I wanted to be sure that they were taken care of. So Thurston would book me in Guthrie, Oklahoma, Woodrow, Oklahoma, and Tulsa and Muskogee. I would go charging in on a big white horse with a big white Stetson.

The odd thing about it was I did a good job. I was amazed. I would get great press wherever I went.

And even though I seemed to have a calling for this kind of work, I did not consider it any kind of betrayal of my dream. But the reality was that I was making more money and making possible a better quality of the life for the Grigsby family.

Eventually, as often happens, opportunities sprang from my job at Thurston. I had a friend who heard me speak at several farm meetings. His name was Bill Bowers and he owned Marco Mills. He bought a lot of stuff from this mill up in Kansas City, called the Fulton Bag and Cotton Mills. That's where their manufacturing plant was located. Somehow my name came up there and the people wanted to talk to me about a job. I talked to them on the phone and they offered me four times what I was making at Thurston.

And that's when I almost made the mistake of placing money ahead of my sports dream. Suddenly, because of that money, that's where I thought I wanted my career to go. So I said, fine, I will come to work for you. The year was 1952.

The family stayed back in Joplin and I went to Kansas City. It cost me $6.25 for a ticket on the Kansas City Southern and off I went to the big city. Once I was here, I plopped down another $4 for a room in the Grund Hotel in Kansas City, Kansas. As you might guess from the name, it was a real fleabag.

I prayed all night long about whether I was doing the right thing. The next morning I went in and they were ready to introduce me to everybody. But before they could say a single word I dropped a big bomb on them. I said, "I'm sorry, I'm not coming to work here!"

"What do you mean? We just brought you here!"

"No, I paid my own way. And I appreciate your faith in me. Thanks, but no thanks!"

Whatever happened to Fulton Bag and Cotton Mills? Is it still around? I don't know. When I walked out the door that's the last time I ever heard anything about it. It could have been gone the next day. I have no idea.

I said sayonara and went to the nearest telephone. I put in a call to Saint Teresa's College. I had a connection there from Joplin, Father James P. Lyons, who had since been sent to Kansas City. He asked me to come out and talk. I ended up talking to Father Lyons and the college president, Mother Berenice O'Neill. She told me she thought the college would like to have me there because they needed somebody with a little fire.

"You can sell our program," I was told.

I was always that way; full of fire and optimism. I just sort of had a happy disposition. And I think Mother Berenice just sensed that. I became, initially, admissions counselor and was paid $300 a month.

I guess I'll really never know for sure whether it was a case of them wanting to do something charitable for me or whether they were going to capitalize on my enthusiasm.

But I do know that the Monsignor also had a liking for me. But Monsignor Arthur Tighe also must have seen the crack I was in. He knew I needed work because he knew I had a wife and kids back in Joplin. In the meantime, he let me live in his parish house, allowing me to get enough money saved to bring Fran and the boys there. I stayed in the rectory with the Monsignor and did everything but hear confessions. The Monsignor had a housekeeper who made great meals, so I also ate pretty well. In any case, the church, through its positive encouragement, convinced me to stay in Kansas City and, in time, it would work out as though it had been a gift from God.

At the same time, I think there was some understanding that I wasn't going to spend my entire life in the college. But I think Monsignor Tighe could see possibilities of me eventually working with the diocesan newspaper, *The Register*. Archbishop Edwin O'Hara wanted me to run the paper advertising.

I was Mr. Everything at the college. If they had a big ceremony, there might be a potted plant on one side of the stage and me on the other. We did that to give it a visual balance, since I really had no other purpose to be up there. If there were a graduation, I'd slip into a cap and gown and be a doctor of laws or something, depending on who was needed for the event. The Archbishop also had a limo, so sometimes I would chauffeur the nuns around.

I also recruited women for nursing at Saint Joseph Hospital and was eventually nominated to the board of the National League of Nursing. It was perfect because I was a guy who couldn't even put a band-aid on, and yet I would go to a convention with 9,000 women…and me.

As it turned out, I got something far more important out of this than simply working for a newspaper and the college. It was considerably more than just a job. There was something planted there at the time. And dealing with those people…

It sort of brought my thinking and my life into focus. It gave me a broader and deeper sense of my life and family, which now included the Catholic Church.

I had never been a Catholic and had never been around the church. I had been an Episcopalian and considered becoming an

Episcopal priest at one point. But when I came to the Catholic Church I dropped all thoughts of that. Working around those nuns, especially the Saint Joseph sisters, was inspiring. They were all college educated and all very smart ladies. And I was able to get a lot from them in terms of further education by just being around them. They had a very fine staff of professors there. I think I learned a lot from all of them. But maybe more than anything else, I learned patience. It gave my life more direction and more of a focus.

And I think Fran picked up on that, too. She, at times, thought they were taking advantage of me because they were always calling me for chauffeuring to wakes; this and that. But then when she thought they might be taking advantage I would get a call from the college and I would run over there and they would have a birthday cake for Fran or something for the kids, and I would bring it home. We would just start laughing about being taken advantage of.

During the early part of our marriage, Fran was very busy with her life. She left me alone. I think she had enough confidence in me and what I could do. That is not to say, though, that we did not have tense times. It was tough. We had eventually moved into a house at 5618 Olive in Kansas City. At the time we paid $85 a month rent. I would try to do the plumbing. I think I stopped up the whole damn neighborhood one time.

I do not think, however, that this put a stress on our marriage. Fran came from a family of eight children. She was very good at sewing. She made the girls' dresses and outfitted the boys. She had two brothers, so she had been around boys and she knew how to handle them pretty well.

We didn't have a lot of money at that time, and absolutely no disposable income.

While working with the Catholic schools I also got to know all of the guys who were coaches in the Catholic high schools. Buddy Bramer was at Rockhurst and about the same time I became close to Eddie and Jimmy Ryan, longtime high school basketball coaches at Rockhurst. I also refereed football with them. By being able to referee I could pick up an extra $15. That was a good way to pay the grocery bill for the next week and a half.

Refereeing was something that I had gotten into long before I had gotten back from World War II. At first I wanted to officiate because I was simply interested in sports. Over the course of the next three decades, it was something that I could do to supplement my family income. It helped my family get through some of those early hard times.

Being a referee on the high school and small college levels for nearly 30 years also greatly affected my reluctance to be too critical of officials once my sports broadcasting career took off. Even today, I consider myself to be among the officiating fraternity and I still have the program of the Neosho Wildcats football game with Mt. Vernon that I did with Lawrence Redd of Cherokee, Kansas, and Max Cherry of Carthage, Missouri. It was one of the first games I refereed and was played at two o'clock the afternoon of November 24, 1948. I vividly recall the game at Neosho High School Stadium.

And how could I forget my entry into Kansas City officiating? A man by the name of Ab Hinshaw literally got me going. He loaned me knickers, socks, a shirt and a jock strap so I could do my first game. I was paid $10 and was extremely nervous because it was a big rivalry game between East and Northeast. I remember that by the end of the game, both schools wanted to kill me.

Of course, just like today, you had to be certified to do any kind of officiating. I had earlier gotten my approval and carried cards from both the Kansas and Missouri State High School Activities Association. When I came to Kansas City, I also was affiliated with the Kansas City Officials' Association. Every time I did games I would receive ratings, and because mine were high, I got all the opportunities to referee that my crowded schedule would allow.

"Bill Grigsby, former Joplin sportscaster, now of Kansas City has become one of the busiest high school football officials in the state..." Porter Wittich wrote in the Joplin *Globe* on October 19, 1954.

Once a hustler, always a hustler, I contend.

Being a referee also had its risks, as I vividly recall from doing a football game at William Jewell College in the mid-sixties. I was the field judge and was running down the sidelines alongside a tight end who had just caught a pass and was going for a touchdown. In those days, I had pretty good speed. I got a little too close while he was swinging his arms and elbows. Wham! All of a sudden his elbow caught me square in the face, and my teeth started flying everywhere. At half time, some of my friends came out of the stands to help me look for my teeth.

The real problem was that I had some TV commercials scheduled for the following Monday, and two of my front teeth were missing. It turned out okay, though. I bought a package of Black Jack gum and made teeth out of it and drew little lines to distinguish what looked like a couple of teeth. On television you couldn't tell the difference. It was perfect.

Norris Patterson, the athletic director and football coach at Jewell, always needled me about that and other things. "I need a couple wins this year, I'm going to put you down to work the game," he would kid me, since we were good friends.

One time in a very critical game I had to call a pass interference on the Cardinals. Jewell ended up losing the game. Afterwards, when I was coming out of the shower, Patterson kept walking back and forth in front of the door glaring at me. He never came in but would just give me this horribly hateful look.

"You got a problem there, Coach?" I finally had to fire back at him.

"Damn you, damn you, Grigsby, why did you have to call that penalty?" he screamed.

"Look, I call 'em the way I see 'em. I don't care if it's William Jewell or Graceland or if you're the coach, that's the way it's going to be. If you don't want me to officiate your games, then fine! And get out of here." He was mad for about a day, and then we were soon heckling each other in jest again.

And just for the record, I never had anything less than an "A" rating, which is as high as you can get.

I also brought my interest in professional wrestling with me when I made the move from Joplin. I had known Carl Applegate in Joplin, who was the promoter there, and he was good enough to introduce me to some of the 'rasslin promoters in KC. Carl sent me to George Simpson, who was then the big promoter of Kansas City wrestling. I signed on as the ring announcer, and trumped up publicity from time to time.

It was a hectic pace, to be sure, working for the Catholic Church, Simpson, and officiating all at the same time. When the phone rang, if I happened to be home, I never knew who would be on the other line, Dick the Bruiser or Mother Berenice. Much to their credit and tolerant nature, the nuns never made me feel uncomfortable about all the different things I was doing to keep my family afloat.

Although some might question my involvement in pro wrestling at the same time I was trying to establish my credability in the community, the opportunity was actually quite beneficial to me. It was the wrestling that taught me a lot about selling a message. I saw it as a challenge. Besides it was fun and just play-acting. I felt like Alice in the looking glass. I walked through the looking glass into this other world and played around in it and came back into the real world several hours later. Five years later I had a show on KMBC-TV called *Show-Me Wrestling*, that came on every Wednesday night at 10:30 that would highlight certain matches.

Could I do this kind of diverse work today? I am not so sure, given the restrictive tone of today's politically correct world.

I also loved the Golden Gloves organization. I spent a lot of time with Joplin kids who were lured off the street into an organized boxing program. It was a great outlet for youngsters who needed some energy corralled. I'm sure it saved hundreds of kids from prison. I think a lot of people think boxing is a brutal sport. To me it wasn't, and I served many years, proudly, as the AAU commissioner for Southwest Missouri, never missing a Golden Gloves event.

Television was also beginning to get a foothold in people's lives about this time.

Kansas City's first TV station was WDAF-TV, which had gone on the air October 16, 1949. *The Kansas City Star* owned the VHF (very high frequency) station in the early years, and Jay Barrington was Channel 4's first sportscaster. Larry Rhea was the city's first TV play-by-play baseball announcer, doing the Kansas City Blues' minor league games.

The second station to sign on was UHF (ultra high frequency), KCTY-TV, Channel 25. It began operations in June of 1953 in the old Pickwick Hotel at 10th and McGee. The station was owned and operated by the Empire Coil Company, which also made the converters that were required to receive UHF signals.

It seemed like a golden opportunity to break into this new media, so I auditioned and was luckily hired. Only at the time it didn't turn out to be such a lucky break. When TV hit the scene in the early 50s, it wasn't clear which modulation, either VHF or UHF, would become the popular choice since UHF required a different converter than most TV sets had back then. Today, of course, both frequencies are very much in use.

But then those questions weren't nearly a concern for me as getting a job in the industry. I was hired by program director Dick Ostrander as sports director and had a thousand ideas to put in motion. When I got my first paycheck, my gross for the week was $148.00, and after taxes I took home $127.74.

Channel 25 was on the old DuMont Network, which also carried National Football League games at that time. Locally, we did some great work, televising boxing, bowling and high school football.

"Sports fans will have their initial taste of high school football on TV," it was written in *The Kansas City Star* on September 27, 1953. "KCTY will telecast the Shawnee Mission-Wyandotte football game this Friday night direct from the Wyandotte Stadium with Bill Grigsby handling the sportscasting."

On Thursday nights I would interview a "famous" wrestling personality, and we had a feature called "Name The Hold" in which wrestlers such as Man Mountain Dean would appear to explain some of the finer techniques of their sport. Viewers would

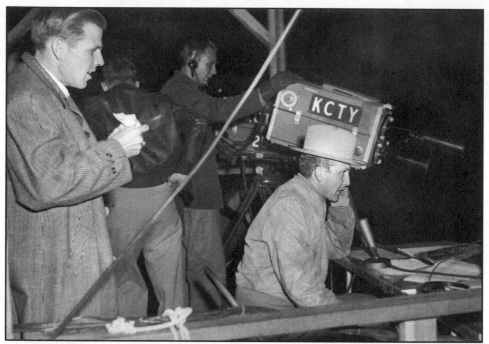

Working an early high school football game on KCTY, Channel 25.

receive free passes to matches at Memorial Hall in Kansas City, Kansas. My favorite hold was the Abdominal Stretch, with the Outside Stepover Toehold a close second.

On other nights I would interview a Golden Gloves personality or maybe Parke Carroll, general manager of the Kansas City Blues baseball team.

In the meantime, all 35 employees worked with management to try to sell potential sponsors time on the station. In the studios we had refrigerators with shrimp, all kinds of great food we would feed the agencies. We had martinis, everything, hoping that agency people would have a drink or two and get drunk and buy some time on the station. They didn't.

We had an old bus that we would drive around for our remotes. Inside was all of our equipment. We would jump in the thing with the camera guys and grips. Some of them were paid, some of them were just volunteers. It was fun. Once we did a high school football game from the roof of the old Municipal Stadium. They found out later the platform where we all were with those heavy, bulky cameras was rotten. We were lucky we didn't fall.

It really looked like the station was going to make it. More and more converters were being sold, or so it seemed, and we were certainly providing a lot of programming.

Things were going great. So much so in fact, that I decided one day I could quit St. Teresa's and my moonlighting at Memorial Hall, where they held the wrestling matches in Kansas City, Kansas. It also meant that the family could get its first car, and I could finally buy my first suit.

I bought a used Pontiac at Eddie Williams Ford, and later in the day, got fitted for my suit. Afterwards, I decided to head over to the office. When I got off the elevator, the switchboard operator told me to go straight to the studio for a meeting.

When I walked in, everybody had a grim look on his or her face.

"The station is shutting down," I was told.

A short article appeared in the morning newspaper.

"The last program was a news and weather show at 9:30 in which a short farewell to Kansas City listeners was read. The announcement of the closing of the station was made by Dr. Allen B. DuMont. A very small percentage of the nearly 400,000 very high frequency receivers in the area were equipped to receive Channel 25, the company said."

I got my last paycheck two days later—a day after my birthday—on Valentine's Day, 1954. Although I couldn't take my suit back, I was able to take the car back. I also was able to convince Mother Berenice and the wrestling folks to take me back.

My short TV career flopped, but not because of my failures. It was a setback, but it did not undermine my desire or confidence to be a sports broadcaster.

Merle Harmon, my buddy from my Western Association broadcasting days, was supportive and promised to keep an eye out for me should any positions arise. While I had given up my job as the Miners' play-by-play guy on WMBH when I had left Joplin,

Merle had also left the Topeka Owls in 1952. He had caught on with the University of Kansas, doing their football and basketball games and, in 1954, also became the radio broadcaster for the Kansas City Blues. Merle was definitely on his way up since the Blues were in the American Association, only a step below the big leagues and the Triple A farm club of the New York Yankees. He and Larry Rhea did the games on WHB, 710 AM.

Later, Merle convinced WDAF radio to let us broadcast a college football Game of the Day. He sold it on a national basis, so the games were carried all over the United States. We did Notre Dame games, Wisconsin and Air Force games. In fact, we did the first ever Army-Air Force football game. It was played in Yankee Stadium.

It was a great boost to my ego, career, and my friendship with Merle Harmon.

Meanwhile, on the home front, Fran was doing a great job of raising the kids. Occasionally, I was able to make a guest appearance, and the kids would ask their mom who the strange man was who had just come through their door.

Once Jimmy asked me what I did for a living, and I was hard pressed to explain it to my young son in a manner that made any sense to me, not to mention him. Even today, after decades of so many twists and turns, the subject is still a bit perplexing to my adult children.

Because of my obsession to take care of my family financially, I was never much of a "honey-do" guy at home. That's not to say, though, that I didn't make an honest effort.

I remember our first television set. One day the picture tube went out and I couldn't afford to have a repairman come out and fix it. So I went out and bought a picture tube, thinking it would be an easy chore to fix it. I made everyone leave though, just in case I blew up the house. Nothing exploded, although I was told later that I could have easily electrocuted myself. I haven't touched a TV, except for the remote, since.

Another time Fran and the kids took a trip and I thought I would help out with some repairs while they were gone. The upstairs sink was slow draining, so I asked the man next door, Fred Jillson, if he had any plumbing equipment.

He said his snake would take care of it. I wasn't sure whether he was talking about a reptile or some kind of tool. In any case, he said it would fix the problem. The only thing it would cost me was two six-packs of beer. A fair trade, I reasoned, and we headed off to solve the problem.

God almighty, this snake of his was long. About 400 yards with big jaws on the end of it. In a former life he had been a plumber, he explained. Anyway, he started shoving the snake down the sink. We were on the second floor, and by the time he was done, he had shoved this thing all the way to Arthur Bryant's, I think.

The only problem is that after he pushed this thing 400 yards down the pipes, it became stuck solid. And by that time he was half gassed from drinking beer. The snake just would not come out. I finally asked him what he planned to do.

"Call a plumber."

"But that's why you're here!" I screamed. "I can't afford a plumber."

So all of a sudden before he could get to a telephone, I reached down and sliced if off with a cutter. He was horrified, but I couldn't have Fran see that big snake sticking out of her sink.

We eventually pulled the drain pipe apart. I had to put everything back together with putty and painted it to make it look like metal, so Fran wouldn't notice. Fred told me it wouldn't work, but I told him it couldn't be helped since that's the way I had to fix the problem. As it turned out, even with all the intervention, the sink was now draining slower than it had been before.

Of course, when Fran got back she found out about the whole escapade. She was quite upset. She complained that I couldn't do anything, and I explained to her that I would never be like her dad who could fix anything. Today, if I even pick up a screwdriver or wrench, she will yank it out of my hand.

I began my association with the Kansas City-based National Association of Intercollegiate Athletics in the early fifties, originating the NAIA Radio Network from the men's basketball tournament at Municipal Auditorium. Over the course of several decades, I broadcast more than 400 games.

I was the guy who did the games for the NAIA teams that were too poor to have their own regular announcers. In one instance, I was made an Honorary Alumnus of Tennessee Wesleyan College of Athens, Tennessee.

"For the exciting world pictures with which you brought the game to those in Athens," my 1967 certificate reads.

I'm also an honorary citizen of Portales, New Mexico.

It expanded my notoriety to places that I had never dreamed even existed. I became a hero in places like Yankton, South Dakota, and Wayne, Nebraska.

"You are a gracious announcer and you made our defeat much less painful with your kind words about Texas and a game bunch of fine boys," wrote a person from Archer City, Texas.

Another letter said, "You said so many nice things about my boy. I didn't know you knew him."

I didn't, of course. But I tried not to let anybody know that and went out of my way to research something about the team's hometown.

"And now you folks back at Cliff's drugstore," I shouted one night near the end of a game, "Get down on your knees. We're going to need help these last two minutes."

I needed very little preparation to do a game broadcast, even if I had never seen either team before. Once they had gone the length of the basketball court, I was able to identify all the players by name.

When I spotted friends at the media table I made mention of them.

"Some of the nation's leading sportswriters are covering the game tonight," I said more than once. "Sitting right down in front of us is Trebor Neztneh. He came clear in from Topeka for this one."

Topeka is less than a 100 miles away, but who's to know that in Oregon? And who was Trebor Neztneh? Spelled backwards it was Bob Hentzen, sports editor of the *Topeka Capital-Journal*.

Even the mighty *Washington Post* came to do a story on this unique skill and opportunity that I had perfected.

"For six days each year," wrote reporter Kenneth Denlinger, "the voice of Middle America is neither Nixon nor Goldwater, Humphrey nor McGovern. It is Bill Grigsby, an enthusiastic radio jockey who rattles out the play-by-play at 250 words a minute, with gusts up to 375."

I also served as the track announcer for the NAIA Indoor Track & Field Championships for many years and served as honorary coach for the national tennis championship when it was held at Kansas City's Rockhill Tennis Club.

I was a strong advocate of the NAIA and was honored by the organization with the Frank Cramer Award in 1972 as the person who had done the most for the men's basketball tournament. But I was humbled in 1991 when the NAIA saw fit to make me a member of its Hall of Fame during a ceremony at the Hyatt Regency Hotel in Kansas City.

Years later, I was honored to also be selected to the first class of inductees to the Missouri Sports Hall of Fame in Springfield. It was quite a group of sports heroes, and I was humbled to be included with the likes of George Brett and Frank White of the Royals and Len Dawson and Otis Taylor of the Chiefs. We were the five Kansas Citians chosen. Others in that initial class were Whitey Herzog and Red Schoendienst of the St. Louis Cardinals, Jackie Smith and Roger Wehrli of the football Cardinals, pro golfer Payne Stewart, bowler Dick Weber and former tight end great Kellen Winslow of Mizzou and the San Diego Chargers. It was a fairytale evening with Bob Costas as Master of Ceremonies.

My scheduled in the mid-fifties also included a freelance contract to do the University of Kansas football and basketball games as well as a taped radio program called *Jayhawk Locker Room Club*.

I got the KU job thanks to a tip from my broadcasting guardian angel, Merle Harmon. He had been doing the Jayhawks

The first class of inductees to the Missouri Sports Hall of Fame. From left, back row: Red Schoendienst, Len Dawson, Roger Wehrli, George Brett, Frank White, the late Payne Stewart, Otis Taylor, Jackie Smith and Whitey Herzog. Second row: John Q. Hammonds and mother of Hale Irwin. Front row: me, Bob Costas and Dick Weber.

but had accepted the play-by-play with the Athletics, who were moving from Philadelphia to Kansas City.

Merle told me to get over to Lawrence as soon as possible to apply. It paid off, and I signed a contract that basically paid me $35 a game and I had to pay my own travel expenses. I was going to get $35 whether the game was in California or Allen Field House.

When I did the football games, my broadcast partner was Dick Harp, who replaced the legendary Phog Allen as KU's basketball coach shortly after the start of the 1956 season.

In fact, I was the announcer for the first game ever at Allen Field House in 1955. The Jayhawks played archrival Kansas State, and Phog had stayed on as the KU coach so he could be on the bench when they dedicated the Field House in his name.

Phog was one of the most interesting sports figures I ever met. I was smoking at the time I was doing the KU games, and Phog, who was also a medical doctor, would always lecture me about the bad image it was for children and how it would hurt my health. One night I pulled into the parking lot at the Field House and pulled up next to Phog sitting alone in his Cadillac.

"Uh, son...I think I smell something burning," he said to me when we greeted each other.

He was acting real funny, but I assumed he thought I had been smoking again and was about to berate me. But as it turned out, Phog had been secretly smoking in his car, and when I pulled up he had tried to put the cigarette out before I caught him.

At half time, there was an announcement that Phog's car had burned up in the parking lot. The cigarette he had tried to put out ended up in the back seat where it caught the car on fire.

The celebrated basketball legend was also known for his lengthy answers to reporters' questions.

When I was doing *Jayhawk Locker Room Club* I asked Phog a rather complicated question by design. As he began his answer, I got up, left the studio and walked downstairs to the Coke machine. I put money in the machine, took a couple swigs and casually went back upstairs. When I walked back in the studio, Phog was still chattering away happily as though I had never left.

It was a rich experience riding the rails with Phog and his star, Wilt Chamberlain. The biggest of thrills was being the voice of the Final Four the first year it was broadcast nationally.

The year was 1957, the same year I also signed on with KMBC radio as a time salesman. Now in my mid-thirties, I was doing exactly what I wanted in life. And it was an exciting time for

Kansas City, with the A's bringing major league baseball to town. It was a time when box seats cost three dollars and a Del Ray, two-door sedan cost $1,775 at Dumas-Milner Chevrolet.

I felt excited for my friend, Merle Harmon, and his new broadcast partner, Ed Edwards, as they prepared to call the action of the Athletics the following spring.

CHAPTER 5

Wrestling

I had gotten a taste of wrestling while I was in Joplin as a kid and later as an adult when I returned from World War II. But like my involvement with the baseball Miners, I jumped from the minor leagues to the big leagues of wrestling when I came to Kansas City in the early 1950s.

My life is very much akin to the television show *Survivor*. Surviving is what I did when I came here, and it was through wrestling I was able to do that. Working for the nuns wasn't enough for Fran and me to raise the two children we now had, so I had to have another source of money coming in. And since I knew a little of the wrestling game, that's naturally where I looked.

I went to the wrestling office over on 39th Street, just off of Main where Orville Brown had his office as a promoter. I convinced him I could do the ring announcing.

"And I can also write, Orville," I told him. "I'll write all your publicity, and when new wrestlers come to town I'll write their stories."

I wrote for a magazine called *The Sportscaster*, but *The Kansas City Star* would only carry a short account and not treat it like a sporting event. That's because a few years earlier, the sports editor, C.E. McBride, had placed a bet on a wrestler, only to be told by the promoter that he should try to get out of the bet because McBride's guy wasn't going to win. McBride was pretty upset to find out the whole thing was fixed.

But even though *The Star* wasn't running anything but a small story, I would take a story down to the paper after the matches. I'd usually get something in, and Orville would be pleased.

When I got involved in wrestling in the fifties, there was a semblance of it being on the level. When people came to the hall, they weren't exactly sure whether it was real or not. Today, of course, there is no doubt. Now it is more of a talking contest or who can scream the loudest.

But let me put it this way: everything in sports is entertainment, so it is always important to keep that mind. People are paying money to be entertained, whether it's wrestling, the Royals or the Chiefs.

There are highs and lows that come with these forms of entertainment. The highs come when you win, the lows when you lose. And it's the same if you take a close look at the fantasy world of wrestling.

I first became aware of wrestling when I was a kid in Joplin and later after I became the Commissioner of the Amateur Athletic Union in that part of the state. So I had to go to many of the wrestling matches as part of my duties. And back then most people went to a wrestling match thinking it was on the level.

Back then we had people like Wild Red Barry and Leroy McQuirk, the junior light heavyweight champion who was out of Tulsa. The thing about Leroy, who was portrayed as the clean-cut, All-American type, is that he only had one eye. He lost an eye in an automobile accident.

Red Barry was a showman from Pittsburgh, Kansas. His gimmick was talking. By the time he retired, he was big in Hollywood.

He might have even been considered a forerunner to Arnold Schwarzenegger. Red made it in Hollywood because he was good with words. He was Muhammad Ali before Ali had invented himself. Ali was big with words before a boxing match, and Red was a lot like that before a wrestling match years before Ali became famous for it.

Red drew people in because of his routine, but he also was a good athlete and wrestler. He got his name, Wild Red, because one day a woman called the Pittsburgh police to say there was a wild man up in a tree, looking like a monkey. Red was actually in the city park, jumping from tree to tree and screaming. He was setting the stage for a lifetime in wrestling...and Hollywood, I guess.

Red was also one of the tightest guys I ever knew. You would go out to dinner with him, and if you looked around after walking away from the meal, you might catch him picking up the tip.

Some of the others were Sailor Morgan, Frank Wolfe, a big evil, militant German guy. Back then I understood the scheme of setting up evil against good. That was my job.

When you think about it, going to a wrestling match is much cheaper than having to go to a psychologist's office. People vent their frustrations and aggravations at a wrestling match. They look at the bad guy as though he's their boss at work.

The American Legion was the sponsoring organization, and as a kid I would go down and mark the ringside seats with chalk to show people where their seats were. My cousin, who had been a Legionnaire, got me involved. As a result I got to know all of these characters, who were all good athletes. I very much enjoyed it, as well as the Golden Gloves, which was on the level. In the beginning, I didn't really know that wrestling wasn't legitimate. At one point I asked an old-time wrestler, Joe Becker, about it.

"Mr. Becker," I said bravely, "when was the first fixed wrestling match?"

"The first time two men got into a fight," he responded. "And if there was any betting on it, you can bet it was fixed!"

But you couldn't exactly describe it as fixed, maybe scripted. Later on when I had come to Kansas City and gotten heavily involved at Memorial Hall in Kansas City, Kansas, I would go into the locker room and explain that the matches would be two falls out of three, and we needed to have this or that happen. The guys, the main headliners anyway, were smart enough to carry it off.

I would also later have an opportunity to work on the great endings to the match. It was the endings that made the wrestling match and kept the people coming back.

It was also a time when they had the great holds. In the early days of Madison Square Garden and the world championship matches, they'd have Jim Londos fighting somebody like Strangler Lewis or Frank Gotch. They'd get a toehold and hold it for an hour!

People would buy that hook, line and sinker…and just sit there watching and almost always yelling at the top of their lungs.

Eventually came the revelation that the thing wasn't all on the up and up. People were shocked, but they still went to see the good guy win. Our premise was not to let the good guy win for about eight weeks, because people would just keep coming back, hoping that the bad guy would lose. But we'd always have the bad guy win in the last couple of seconds on some strange call, which upset people even more. It was very much acting, like a soap opera.

There was one wrestler by the name of Lou Plummer, a guy with a great big, massive chest. He came to me one day and wanted me to get him on the television show, *The $64,000 Question*.

"I'll try Lou, but what would be your category?" I asked.

"The Bible," he said without hesitation. "I guarantee you that when they find out that I'm a big-time wrestler and that my specialty is the Bible they'll put me on national TV and put me over."

"Put me over" was a term we used in wrestling that meant that he was predetermined to be the winner. It meant that they would be feeding him the questions…and the answers.

I did have a contact at the network, and after I made the call, sure enough, Lou was called and became one of the contestants. As he predicted, he began to win. He advanced all the way to the finals. But on the very last question, they must have pulled the rug out from under him. The answer was not provided.

I remember seeing him on TV in that isolation booth at the end when the camera zoomed in on him after they gave him the last question. Sweat was pouring out of him, and he didn't end up winning the big money.

But he did prove to me that the quiz shows were phony because they had "put him over." Until the final question anyway. Of course, he was smart enough not to complain.

One night I asked Lou for a favor.

"Lou, you've never done the chloroform ending here for me, would you do it tonight?" I requested. "I've heard it's really an exciting finish."

"Bill, I'm not quite quick enough any more. People are likely to kill me before I'd get to the locker room."

But about three weeks later he came to me and said he would do it if I did one thing for him.

"When it all hits the fan, I'll be coming over the top (of the ropes) and I want you to block the first guy that tries to get to me. If you don't I'm liable to go under a pile of humanity."

So the match is underway and Plummer is his usual rotten self. But he loses the first fall. He complains to Lou Spandel, the referee, that he has hurt his knee and that he needs to go to the locker room to get a wrap.

"Yeah, go ahead," Spandel tells him.

A short time later, Plummer is coming back into the hall where the 4,000 people are going nuts. Even I can smell the ether as he's coming back in. He's got this rag down in his trunks that he has soaked in ether. Nevertheless, we start the second fall and after he gets Richard Brown in a headlock, Plummer reaches down in his trunks, pulls this rag out, and puts it on Richard's nose. Brown does a half-twist and down he goes onto the canvas, completely out.

The whole trick to the stunt, though, is that the fans have to know that it was trickery, so they'll be angry. So Plummer drops the rag and kicks it into ringside right in front of two little old ladies. As soon as that thing hit, one of them yells out at the top of her lungs, "My God, he's been chloroformed!"

When she said that, it was the signal, and Lou came flying over the top of the ropes. And as I promised, I gave the first guy to come after him a body block, and Lou headed to the locker room untouched.

That was the chloroform ending.

The wrestling biz in the early days operated pretty much as an area consortium. For instance, if I were a promoter in New York, I would have about 50 wrestlers in my stable. If you went to Indianapolis, there would be another guy there who would have his wrestlers. And the same was true in Cincinnati or Chicago or Kansas City.

They would all have an understanding who would be the world champion. But they always picked a guy who was a tremendous athlete with a good body and a good, clean reputation. The key, though, was to create the big rivalries or the good versus evil scenarios.

Orville Brown was the guy in Kansas City, a friend of mine whom I worked for. Orville, when he was wrestling, was a big farm boy and, I mean, he was tough. He and Bobby Bruns would go at it and the people loved it. Everybody thought that Bruns and Orville hated each other. But they were simply great actors, not to mention friends.

One night the two of them wrestled in St. Joseph, Missouri to a full house. What people didn't know was they had come together in the same car. After putting on great show, they headed back to Kansas City. They came up over a hill going about 80 miles an hour. On the other side of that hill, a tractor-trailer had jack-knifed across the road. They crashed into the side of it, the car being wedged underneath.

Had it not been for the fact that both of them had been in such great shape and so strong, it would have killed them. As it was, a big part of Orville's skull was opened up, leaving him terribly injured. It had been planned that he was going to be the next world champion, but because he lost much of the use of one of his arms, it didn't happen. It was a shame, because he was such a great man and was so highly respected. Since he could not wrestle any more, he took over as a promoter.

One night I was doing the ring announcing and we had The Sheik come to town with all his tunics and garb. He had everything but a camel. We had 10,000 people there that night and the guy who was supposed to wrestle him couldn't make it for some reason. So we recruited some former football player from Kansas State, who was going to be the "victim" for The Sheik that night.

"Gooooood evening, ladieeeees and gentlemeeeen," I began. "Please welcome The Sheik and his opponent. Ranked third in the world and one of the great upcoming heavyweights…"

I introduced the sub, and as I jumped off the ring apron the crowd was roaring. Landon Laird, who wrote the "About Town" column for *The Star*, said to me, "Grigsby, you lied to those people!"

I said, "Landon…wrestling is a lie!"

The Sheik put on quite a show that night. He even had little eyeballs carved out of wood and he'd make it look like he was gouging people's eyes out, then throw them out to the crowd.

Later that same year, The Sheik was back, and again we had a big crowd. After the match, which he had won, the crowd wouldn't leave because they were still angry. There were about 50 rednecks at ringside, and every one of them wanted a piece of The Sheik. I could tell he was a little bit frantic trying to figure out how in the world he was going to get back to the locker room without getting killed. Of course, he wasn't a sheik at all, but some guy from Cleveland who looked good in a robe.

Finally, since he was a good athlete, he vaulted over the top rope and hit the ground running. The chase was then on, with a mob of rednecks chasing after him. He bolted straight for the doors, but he had picked the wrong one, and all of a sudden he found himself outside in the eight degree weather with the wind whistling. It was 11 o'clock at night and he was on 13th Street. I quickly ran up the ramp and watched as he was tearing down the street with his robes blowing and yelling, "TAXI…TAXI!" It was a scene out of a Mel Brooks movie.

He was staying, of all places, at the Aladdin Hotel.

There are many tricks of the trade in wrestling that have not been disclosed freely, except in the inner circles of the game.

All that blood you sometimes see? Chicken blood. Little capsules of it. For instance, when a guy would get knocked out of the ring, the wrestler still up in the ring would create a diversion while the guy down below is pulling the capsule out of his trunks and smearing the blood all over his face. The crowd would then go crazy.

But, of course, guys really would get hurt every once in a while because they'd be making flying tackles or performing similar physical tactics.

There was also a person known as an "enforcer" in each of the regions. And if one of the guys did break the unwritten rules or vary too much from the plan...or even went after someone on the level...then the "enforcer" would come in and take care of it.

There was no talking; the enforcer would wrestle the violator. That's the way they kept people in line.

But there was little use of enforcers, because it was a great group of guys to be around. They were all mostly college guys who had wrestled at that level or even played football on the collegiate level.

In wrestling, you kind of looked at what was going on in the world, and created related situations for the ring. For instance, after World War II you might take a big guy who had played football and give him some kind of German name. That's how we created Otto Van Krupp, who was a perfect model of a Nazi. He was a big, strong, Arian type with short-cropped blond hair. He even had a leather jacket and jack boots and would goosestep around the ring before the match.

Often the matches were sponsored by the Veterans of Foreign Wars, and some of those guys would go crazy when Otto would parade around. Oh, did they ever want a piece of that guy. They wanted Otto Van Krupp dead. It made it worst when he'd win every week. The feeling kept growing stronger and stronger.

But the truth be known, Otto Van Krupp was actually a Jewish kid from New Jersey. He obviously was also a great actor.

I wouldn't actually write a play-by-play script so much as I would create these scenarios. Orville would say this is what we want to do, and since I had a good imagination I was able to create it.

Another one of my creations was Baby Doe, the midget woman wrestler. It was a character built around a woman who supposedly had been born in Cairo, Egypt. Her mother was a Russian and her father a visiting seaman. Eventually, as the story went, they settled down in Johannesburg, South Africa. Life was going smoothly for Baby Doe until her eighth birthday when her parents were killed in an auto accident. She went to an orphanage, where she stayed until the age of 16.

After wandering through Johannesburg aimlessly, she finally convinced a promoter to establish a Midget Woman World Championship Wrestling Tournament, which Baby Doe wins. But the story gets even better. Baby Doe becomes the darling of European royalty but makes her way to North America where she is booked to wrestle in Memorial Hall.

The crowd was completely taken in by the whole bit, except for one guy who had recognized her from the nearby Armourdale neighborhood where she lived.

I guess I could have done some things better on that one. But remember, this business of pro wrestling was a fantasy world. But it was my survival that was at stake in those days. My deal was that I got three percent of the gate after expenses. I would actually count the crowd. On the average, I would get between $33 and $35 a week. That bought a lot of groceries back in the fifties. I was also refereeing football at the same time, and that brought in another $15 to $20 a game. When you added it all together, Grigs was able to feed the family.

I didn't get out of wrestling promotion until the early 1960s, but it wasn't because I was seen as a con man or anything like that. I did get an occasional letter, though, from people who had accused me of selling out to the wrestling gang.

I finally got out because I was getting enough money from other things, and I simply didn't have the time any more. There were only so many hours in the day. After all, at one time I was doing the wrestling and the refereeing, public speaking, baseball broadcasting and working for the Schlitz Brewing Company.

Pro wrestling today is a more major production than it was then. But I have no regrets about getting out when I did, mainly because I didn't really have the big-time connections that one needs to be in today's wrestling network.

Bob Geigel did well as a former NCAA national champion wrestler. Bob was great when he got involved in pro wrestling because he had a sense of humor. I worked the TV shows with him. He'd grab me around the head, and I thought he might kill me. One time the promoter, George Simpson, thought he was going to.

We were doing a TV show and I said I hoped that children weren't watching the match because of this rotten person who had been such a great college athlete. I told everyone that what he had done during his TV match didn't have any place in sports of any kind.

With that, he grabbed me, put a headlock on me and said, "I'm going to get you, you chicken-necked so and so."

It wasn't planned, but Bob was pretty good at that kind of stuff. To this day we're still very dear friends.

Tommy O'Toole was another good friend and a Canadian wrestler. In 1958 I was living in south Kansas City and was moving. I didn't have any money to move with a big van so I asked Tommy if he'd help me. He came over and by himself picked up the stove and refrigerator and moved them for me. Tommy liked to drink, so I ended up giving him a fifth of whiskey. He drank most of it before he got a call from a St. Joseph, Missouri promoter who wanted him to fill in on a match. I found out later that it was one of the shortest matches on record, because he got over there and simply collapsed.

Then there were the Zaharias brothers. George was the husband of Babe Zaharias, the famous golfer. They wrestled here, and I remember how mean they were. In fact, it was Tommy Zaharias who became known for kidnapping Baby Doe from Orville Brown. Tommy took her on tour for himself and Orville was so upset he got a warrant for Tommy's arrest for stealing his talent. That wasn't for show, it was real.

Just like the cauliflower ears.

All the wrestlers had them back them. It's just what happened when they would wrestle night after night and they'd get each other in headlocks. Calcium would build up to the point that eventually doctors would have to make a pin hole in their ears so they could hear.

I remember a guy by the name of the Swedish Angel, who had a very large head and big cauliflower ears. He'd scare the little kids by just showing up. One day, the Swedish Angel died and I was asked to be one of the pallbearers. I was the only one of the pallbearers who had regular ears.

The Swedish Angel, Wild Red Barry, Nature Boy, Gene Stanley, Baby Doe…the list of unusual characters seemed endless. Dr. Lee Grabel was really popular with women and kids. Dr. Grabel would hypnotize people before matches. They loved him until we teamed him up with Lou Plummer on a tag team. People just couldn't understand why a good doctor would get involved with an evil person like Plummer. Dr. Grabel would hypnotize Plummer before the match, and Lou would pretend he was a robot. He'd come out of the locker room like that and nobody could even talk to him. The doctor had made a monster out of him. When Plummer would get in the ring, his opponent would come running at him, and then just bounce off him.

But one night, the spell wore off and Plummer got hurt. Lou was lying in the middle of the ring, screaming, "Doc! Doc! Doc!" All of a sudden, though, Plummer started stiffening up. I looked across the arena, and Dr. Grabel was there with a flashlight, waving it back and forth.

One night at the end of a match, Nature Boy and Gene Stanley and the Zaharias Boys were supposed to have a confrontation in the ring about the prize money. But everything kind of fell apart and the crowd got all hot and bothered. Afterwards, I went down to the locker room and Nature Boy confronted me.

"Grigsby, I'll never wrestle in Kansas City ever again."

These guys were something. Sometimes they just couldn't remember how it was supposed to end.

It was amazing that the fans bought that stuff. And you'd see every kind of person there: bankers, lawyers, and little old ladies.

Gene Stanlee, who had been Mr. America at one time, was one of the good guys and was a tag-team partner of Nature Boy. We matched them once with the Dusek Brothers, who had been football players up in Nebraska.

There was a pot of money, something like $5,000, going to the winning team. The thing fell apart at the end and it didn't turn out like we had planned. Nature Boy and Stanley had believed they were supposed to win, but they didn't, and a genuine riot broke out in the Hall. The police ultimately had to be called in to quiet things down. None of it had been planned, but I loved it, because you couldn't have created such excitement. When I went down to the locker room, the Dusek brothers were playing cards and Nature Boy was in the shower.

Today's wrestling headliners make millions. Back then, a headliner could expect to get about $250 a night. But, hey, if you wrestled five nights a week, that wasn't all that bad back then.

The toughest part about pro wrestling was the driving. They never went to the little towns, they all had to hit the big cities. You might wrestle Kansas City one night, then Denver, and then swing back and go to Omaha. They'd all be driving together, heading down the highway at 80 miles an hour.

Hillbilly Calhoun was another main draw back then. Later he changed his name to Haystack Calhoun when he was on top at the Madison Square Garden for 13 straight weeks. He was so fat—about 400 pounds—we had to get him stretch jewelry. We dressed him in bib overalls and clodhopper shoes. His gimmick was that he'd simply sit on his opponents and beat on them with his shoes. He'd pack the house with kids, who really seemed to take a liking to him.

I also wrote his life story, and had described him as illiterate. He'd come from the hills of Arkansas, I said. But he made me look bad when he was first starting out, because when he got up in the ring he was signing autographs for all the kids.

"You can't write!" I whispered to him. "Don't you remember you're illiterate?"

From that point on, he'd sign an X whenever somebody wanted his autograph. Actually he was so dumb we had to get rid of him. But the next thing I knew he was in New York City wrestling in the main event in Madison Square Garden and making the big money…$2,500 a match.

A couple months afterwards when I had gone back to do a baseball game I spotted this guy, Haystack, with his wife at a restaurant. As I was walking out, he spotted me and came over and just engulfed me.

"You made my life!" he tells me. "You made it possible for me to be big time."

It was just another example of how everything I've been involved with has worked out. Everything I feel I've been involved with I've been enthusiastic about. Haystack…Baby Doe…and another wrestler by the name of Little Beaver all are success stories.

Not too long ago I ran into one of the sons of Lord Beaverbrook, another creation. It was great retelling some of the tales. Lord Beaverbrook was a guy who we'd dress up in a tux and a monocular before sending him into the ring.

Gorgeous George was George Wagner. He was pretty much a drunk before he came up with a gimmick of having his hair in a permanent wave. It was a good act. He was a lot like the Liberace of wrestling.

But there also was wrestling, good wrestling. Now that's not to say I believe the earlier era of wrestling was more legitimate than it is today with the groups like World Wrestling Entertainment. Like today, back then the end result was really never in doubt. But the big difference between today and then, is that you really did have good wrestlers then. That, in itself, was more fun I believe. They put a lot into what they did and would occasionally get hurt.

The big change came with television. Wrestling, because of the TV broadcasts, became about special effects. It is no longer the wrestling, but the peripheral stuff going on around it that doesn't mean anything. Pro wrestling lost a lot of the glitter of putting on a stage show. Oh, there are some guys—and girls—with great bodies, but where are the drop kicks and techniques that have at least a pretense of legitimate wrestling? Today's people are climbing in and out of the ring and big-bosomed girls are at ringside. Where are the holds? Today they simply get something and hit the other wrestler over the head. It's lost a lot of the glamour for me. No great story lines, no great personalities.

I had a lot of friends that I made in that business, most of whom are dead now. But they were great guys...ones like Bob Geigle. I think the world of him. He is a good person and has been a good person for the Midwest.

It was all built on fantasy and human behavior. It was based on life. There was the good and the bad. It was like going to an opera, a soap opera.

I love traveling, especially when you run into good friends like Sandy Berkley and Tom Landry. Here we are in Rome.

CHAPTER 6

The A's

It was the best of times; it was the worst of times.
In 1958, a lifelong dream came to fruition when I began doing
the Kansas City Athletics' game broadcasts with my longtime
friend Merle Harmon on the Schlitz baseball network. At the end
of the 1961 season, both of us quit our dream jobs rather than put
up any longer with a nightmare owner named Charles O. Finley.

Thanks in large measure to Merle's endorsement, I began my
career as a major league broadcaster at midseason when Ed
Edwards suddenly resigned under growing public criticism of his
style. Even though there was intense public scrutiny after Ed's
departure, I had no hesitation in taking the job. First, it had
become a goal of mine since I was a kid, pretending to broadcast
games in my bedroom. Secondly, it was a no-brainer financially. As
the University of Kansas play-by-play man I was making the
whopping sum of $35 a game besides selling time at KMBC radio,
which later would become KMBZ. With the A's I would eventually receive an annual contract for $12,600. That may not be

impressive by today's megabuck standards, but remember this was the late fifties. The contract didn't put me on easy street, but it went a long way in giving my family middle-class security.

As Edwards bitterly discovered, doing the A's games was no bed of roses. Because the team was so bad it was instead a daily dose of thorns. In the late fifties and early sixties, there was little baseball on television, so consequently, the radio audience on KMBC-AM 980 was huge and vocal. Since the audience didn't have sports talk radio to vent its frustrations, people back then wrote critical letters a lot more often. More often than not they related the quality of the team on the field to the quality of the play-by-play guys in the broadcast booth. The A's struggled, and a mountain of hate mail went to sponsors, the club and the broadcasters. Merle, who had been with the network since its origination in 1954, had more broadcasting experience than Ed. So it was Edwards who became the focus of the frustration. The fans had to take it out on somebody, and it was Ed Edwards. I hoped I wouldn't replace Ed in that way, too.

The sad thing was that it got so bad that Ed was also getting death threats. As a result he became fixated that someone was going to actually poison him. He became paranoid, and he got to the point he wouldn't eat food in a restaurant unless somebody tested it first. It was only a matter of time before he started losing weight, and as his health deteriorated, so too did his air work.

Ed had come from Buffalo, New York, where he had been broadcasting minor league games. Back then it was a huge jump going from the minor leagues to the majors, because there was so much competition for the major league jobs. Remember, there were only eight American League teams and eight National League clubs. It wasn't like today when you have a proliferation of cable and commercial TV and radio broadcasts with three guys in the booth for every game. It's easy to be mediocre and hide amongst the sheer number of broadcasters. There are probably 400 baseball broadcasters today, compared to the 30 or so back then.

Guy Patterson of Majestic Advertising, the agency that was in charge of the broadcasts for the Schlitz Brewing Company, ultimately made the decision to dump Edwards, who publicly said he was leaving to buy a radio station. It was a difficult decision for Guy because Merle was very supportive of his partner as was Ed Sheppard, the broadcast engineer. After a while, though, Patterson came to the realization that it was not only in the best interest of the broadcasts but for Ed's health, which was quickly going down hill.

I was aware of the public criticism of Edwards at the time but had no idea that his job was in jeopardy. I got a call on July 28, 1958, from Patterson indicating that Ed was out and they wanted me to step in to finish out the rest of the season. They indicated that it would be something of a trial run, and if I did well that I would get a contract for the 1959 season.

I'll never forget the date when Guy called, because my calendar that day read, "Every Dog Has His Day!"

The brass at KMBC assured me they supported me doing the games and that they would have people service my accounts while I was on the road with the team since this was only an interim deal. So why, then, wouldn't I have given it a shot, especially since this had always been my dream?

There was a funny headline in *The Star* when the announcement was made on July 30.

"Grigsby Is Named To Broadcast A's, A Veteran In Air Sports."

It made it sound as though I had been broadcasting the antics of stunt pilots.

I went into the baseball broadcasts ecstatic, especially after I had come to the conclusion that I was never going to get a shot at the major leagues. At age 36, I thought I had become too old. I had given up, especially since Fran and I had already decided that we did not want to leave Kansas City. I had narrowed my choice only to the A's and possibly the St. Louis Cardinals.

The first night I went to the park, I was understandably nervous. I was like Annika Sorenstam, walking into a situation that I wasn't real confident about. There have been very few times in my life when I was nervous, but I suspect it showed that night because

I had wanted this so badly. I knew this was my one chance, and I knew I was only going to get this one.

And as luck would have it, my first night at Municipal Stadium the A's were playing the New York Yankees. There was only a slight partition between the two broadcast booths. When I arrived that night, I knew it was the great Mel Allen who was just next door. What a thrill! It made old Grigs feel like he had finally made it.

Merle did the first two innings of the game, and I did the third and fourth before rain came pounding down on us. It came streaming down the stadium steps and right into the booth because there was really no other place for it to go. I think it was the worst rain I can ever remember for a sporting event.

I could hear Allen next door screaming for the Coast Guard to be sent in to rescue him. I was worried because of all of our electrical equipment. I couldn't help but think about this being my very first broadcast and I might get electrocuted. But I figured if that happened, I was at least going to die happy.

Of course, in the late fifties it was Arnold Johnson who was still the owner of the club. Park Carroll was the general manager and was considered very ethical. The manager was my old buddy from the Joplin Miners, Harry Craft. Harry had taken over for his longtime friend, Lou Bouderau. Lou was the first manager of the Kansas City A's but couldn't produce a winner in the early going. Once, after Harry had taken over, the A's were on a road trip to New York and when he got off the bus in front of the team's hotel Harry was approached by a young reporter by the name of Howard Cosell.

"Tell me Craft, how does it feel to take your best friend's job?" Howard quipped.

Even then Howard Cosell was an abrasive personality working for a New York newspaper. We had to restrain Harry.

But the fact remains that the club wasn't all that good nor was I as Merle's sidekick that first half season. My style today and then is completely different. I am a heck of a lot looser now than I was when I first started doing the A's. I think I was trying too hard and was simply pressing.

Frank House might have been the best player we had. He was one of the first guys to ever get a fairly sizable bonus after playing for Detroit. I think he received something like $40,000 to sign, which would only be chump change today. Ned Garver was the ace of the pitching staff, having come over from Philadelphia where he had played for Connie Mack.

Attendance at Municipal Stadium wasn't all that good. When a fan would call to ask when the games started, A's officials would respond, "What time can you get here?" It was a running gag back then.

If the baseball wasn't all that good, at least it was a hoot traveling with this bunch of guys. Bob Swift and Don Hefner were Harry's coaches. After games, we would hit the bar for a little balm for having to be associated with such a bad team. Swift drank Cutty and Harry guzzled VO. We also drank a bit while traveling. It wasn't like it is today when you get on a jet and arrive very quickly. Back then we were either on prop airplanes or even trains when we were on the East Coast.

A lot of times, Joe McGuff, the baseball beat writer for *The Kansas City Star* at the time, would get up a gin rummy game on the trip from KC to Chicago. We would catch the train at Union Station at 6 p.m. and travel all night to Chicago, playing cards the entire night. It was so much more relaxing than the routine today.

By the end of that first season in 1958 I felt I was improving greatly and was hopeful my contract would be renewed for the 1959 season. I kept thinking about what an old umpire, Joe Becker, had told me many years before when I was doing the Joplin games.

"Remember, young man, you're a recorder of events, not a molder of public opinion…just do your job," Becker had stressed to me.

And in all my years of sports broadcasting those words have reverberated in my head. And I guess that's one of the reasons why I have always been reluctant to criticize managers or coaches.

When the season finally came to a merciful end in 1958 I was still uncertain about my future in the A's broadcast booth with

Merle. I know he wanted me back, and I was hopeful that that was because of my talent as much as it was for our friendship.

As it turned out, I had another good friend in Bob Busby, the assistant sports editor for *The Kansas City Star*.

Buzz wrote a column called "On The Level," and made a very supportive endorsement of me during the off season that I believe to be one of the most significant breaks in my life. The headline read, "A Hand to Bill Grigsby."

Busby and I had known each other only casually through the media, but his words that morning in the newspaper forever put me in his favor.

"...Merle Harmon, the veteran member of the (broadcast) team, is in solidly as far as is known, and rightly so. Grigsby's case is different. He was jerked cold off the bench, so to speak, and sent in to replace Ed Edwards.

"For some reason sports broadcasters are in a peculiar position in that they are either violently liked or disliked. Our personal opinion leans us toward the broadcaster who 'reports' what is going on, avoids hysteria, lets the umpires handle the game and keeps the alibis to a minimum. We do not care whether his voice is high, medium or low, so long as he fills the other requirements. Grigsby, in our book, did an excellent job in a tough situation. He knew he was only an interim 'voice' and now his future fate as a baseball broadcaster is up to his sponsor.

"For whatever it's worth, we think he deserves every consideration. He is a good factual reporter of the game."

Buzz passed away in the eighties, but he remains forever in my heart.

On January 14, 1959, another headline appeared in *The Star*. "Grigsby Named for A's."

And on January 23, a week later, I received my new A's contract. It was as though I had just gotten a biopsy back, and I was free of cancer.

That $12,600 salary was huge. It enabled me to buy a car and a house. I paid $11,000 for the home and our payments were $100 a month. It was a wonderful house and accommodated our growing family very nicely.

It also meant that I didn't have to go to the clothing store and get a revolving credit account to get a suit. I could buy clothes for me and my family.

Since I got my contract in mid-winter, I spent the next couple of months doing public speaking on behalf of the team and the sponsors. Obviously, I had to leave my job at KMBC because the broadcasts were moving to WDAF-AM, 610.

My contract also called for numerous other responsibilities beyond just calling the games. I was required to work as a public relations representative for Majestic and to make "any number of personal appearances." Merle and I also had to do commercials for Schlitz, which was the major sponsor of the broadcasts.

We did three, 30-second commercials, and every time we did them, a guy from Milwaukee would fly in to oversee the shoots. The guy would bring 100 cases of beer out to the location and we would do a lot of pouring. If they didn't like the way the beer was poured, we'd have to do another…and another. We went through a lot of stagehands because most of them would drink what we weren't using. On the average, we went through one stagehand about every two hours.

Like Bob Busby had written, I got a lot of feedback when I replaced Edwards. Some people thought my voice was too high and I was aware of those comments the next spring when we went to West Palm Beach for spring training. I started working on trying to lower my voice, which probably was not the thing to do.

By the time the first game rolled around, I had worked out a lower pitch. It was very deep and very stiff. So much, in fact, that after the first game Guy Patterson called the broadcast booth to see who had come in to do the games with Merle.

"That was Bill," Merle told Patterson.

"Come on, Merle, I'm no fool. That was not Bill Grigsby."

"Well, I don't like that other guy, whoever he was. We bought Bill Grigsby and that's the voice we want."

Patterson's response actually made me feel better and taught me a lesson. You've got to be yourself when you do a broadcast. No one ever complained about my voice after that. I supposed I loosened up considerably and that helped my confidence.

Patterson was a guy who could really play some mind games. He liked to go to a bar called Gigi's, and one day asked if I might mention them on the air because they sold a lot of Schlitz there. He knew he couldn't ask Merle to do it because Merle was too straight and didn't drink.

So during the broadcast I said something to the effect, "Hey, Merle, you wouldn't believe who I saw at Gigi's the other night." Well, I found out a short time after I did it that Patterson had made a bet with somebody that he could get me to mention the place on the air. Pretty rotten.

But then again, this was the age of characters. Besides Patterson, who was a master, there was Dr. Nigro and the Pete Carters of the world.

D.M. Nigro was the downtown doctor and was always looking out for Harry. It was about halfway through the '59 season when Harry started drinking a little more because the team was playing a little worse. Sometimes, Harry would be over in the dugout, curled up in sort of a fetal position. Nobody wanted to say much about it, and they just let Doc handle it.

Another time when we were coming home from an especially disastrous road trip, Harry was getting off the airplane and collapsed. Doc gathered him up and stuffed him in a limo and rushed him over to his clinic.

Just to make it look like it had been a medical condition, Dr. Nigro kept Harry in his clinic a couple nights while Bob Swift, the third base coach, did the managing. Well, the timing was interesting because the A's started winning...and winning in most peculiar ways.

The team put together quite a winning streak, making it impossible for Harry to come back or even leave Doc's clinic. It was also about this time when Roger Maris started really making a name for himself. Swift, meanwhile, was being touted as the savior of mankind. Harry, though, was getting real sick of the whole thing but knew if he came out to the stadium, people would lambaste him. So what did he do? He got Doc and I to go over to the clinic in a laundry truck. We backed it up to the door and Harry climbed in so nobody would see him. We took him back to the Phillips Hotel to his room where he could at least get a drink.

A day or so later, there was a paperboy selling *The Kansas City Star* on a downtown corner near the Phillips. He was barking, "Read all about it, Harry Craft out as A's manager."

Well, there was no air conditioning in those days, and Harry had his window wide open and could hear this from his room. He sent a bellman out to get a paper, but when it was delivered to Harry there was no mention of him being fired as the A's manager. The paperboy was just doing that hoping to sell more papers.

In the end, the A's won 11 straight under Swift, and Maris had raised his batting average to something like .340.

It was a stretch that haunted Harry but made Merle and I very popular with the fans, who always feel better about the broadcasters when the team is winning. You can put a lot into your games when a team is winning 11 straight.

The streak ended when the Yankees came to town. It doesn't make any difference whether it's 1959 or 2004; the Yankees always come to town with a real aura. The two teams opened with a double header and the Yanks won both, setting Harry free from his bondage at the Phillips Hotel. Swift went back to coaching, which made him happy because he hadn't been used to the pressure that comes with managing. The bottom line was that we started losing again, but, at least, we were all one big, happy family again. The only problem is that the A's then proceeded to lose 13 straight and Harry did get fired. That's baseball.

Hank Bauer was hired to manage. He was just finishing up his playing career and had the mentality of a player. He worked hard at learning the ins and outs as a manager and kept both Swift and Hefner on as coaches.

During this era, the A's actually had some pretty good ball players. Players like Hector Lopez, Vic Power, Ralph Terry, Suitcase Simpson, Murray Dixon and Bob Cerv who had been a football player out of Nebraska. Cerv hit the ball longer and harder than anybody I have ever seen and broke a lot of windshields in Sam's Parking out in left field.

Probably our best pitcher during my time was a guy named Bud Daley, who twice won 16 games for the A's.

Eventually, all the good ball players ended up going to the Yankees, though. It was a travesty, because if the club could have kept some of those young ball players, the A's would have been a contender in the American League. When you hear that Kansas City was simply a farm club for the Yankees, that is 100 percent accurate. How sad is that for major league baseball that something like that was happening, and nobody did anything about it? Neither Merle nor I could talk about it much, because that would have been hitting too close to home and getting too close to molding public opinion. We were there to simply report the games.

Somewhere along the line, Arnold Johnson had been in business with Del Web of the Yankees. Somehow, Del had a hammer over Johnson because all Web would have to do is call up and say, "Hey, send me Hector....or whoever."

That's how Jerry Lumpe, Hank Bauer, Marv Thornberry and Norm Stevens eventually came to Kansas City...through the New York pipeline. They were descending in their careers.

And that's exactly what happened with Maris, who came to Kansas City from Cleveland in a deal because the Indians refused to send him directly to New York. But at least we got to see him here for a while. He was a fine young man from South Dakota but pretty raw while he was here.

The Yankees had the A's number in more ways than one. At one point, Kansas City had lost 21 straight times to the Yankees. The only way the A's were finally able to break the streak is through trickery.

In the 22nd game, the A's were leading 1-0 with two outs in the bottom of the ninth inning. Pitcher John Tsitouris, however, pitched himself into a jam, loading the bases and facing Mickey Mantle at the plate. Tsitouris called time out to seek advice from the catcher about how to throw to Mick.

"Throw anything you want. I don't want the guilt on me," came the reply.

The two, noting that Mantle was "dug in at the plate all the way to his waist," decided to hatch a plot that might fake out

Mantle and the umpire. Under the plan, Tsitouris was going to fake a pitch to the plate.

So there it was, two outs in the ninth with Mantle at the plate. You could hear a pin drop. Tsitouris goes into his wind-up, acts like he throws the pitch, and the catcher pops his glove as loud as he can as though it's just been hit with the pitch.

The ump screams out, "Strike three, yer out."

Mantle goes nuts, throws his bat into the upper deck and his helmet into the dugout and says, "Ump, that pitch was three feet outside and you know it."

That was one of the exciting games. Unfortunately there were too many of the other kind, the boring kind. But despite the dismal play most of the time, I always strived to maintain a high level of enthusiasm, which wasn't always easy.

When we did the West Coast games, there was a two-hour delay, so the games wouldn't be broadcast back home until 10 o'clock at night. It was the A's fan's sleeping pill. People used to take their radios to bed with them to help get to sleep. I remember calling a double play once and said, "If you're scoring in bed, that went 6-4-3."

You never knew what was going to come out of your mouth.

During the off season, I again did a lot of promotional work for Schlitz. I worked hard for them and it would later pay off handsomely when Merle and I ran afoul of Charlie O. I did a lot of public speaking, charity work, the pro wrestling and the NAIA games. Doing the NAIA basketball tournament in the spring at Municipal Auditorium was very enjoyable because by this time I had gained notoriety for being the A's broadcaster. I was gaining a following and people were beginning to ask me for autographs. But to my family I was simply dad, which was perfectly OK with me.

Arnold Johnson was not a baseball man, but a business type. He was more CEO than anything. I liked him and his wife, Carmen. They had an absolutely glorious place on a jungle-like road in Palm Beach, Florida. That's where he stayed most of the time and was pretty much an absentee owner.

Johnson's last season to own the team was 1960. During spring training of that year he was at the ballpark in West Palm Beach when Ed Vollers, his attorney, brought him divorce papers to examine. Unfortunately, Arnold Johnson suffered a heart attack and died. Carmen got the A's!

The season was very uncertain in terms of the ownership. It was common knowledge that Carmen was wrangling for a buyer and perhaps even negotiating with someone. Nobody seemed to know much about what was going on or who might eventually buy the club. Everyone with the team, though, was leery about anybody new because it might bring change.

When Charles O. Finley's name emerged, all we really knew was that he sold insurance in Chicago and that he was a serious possibility. But no one knew much more about him, so there wasn't this great worry about what kind of changes might be in store.

In time, it was Finley who bought the club from Carmen. He got a great deal, too.

When Finley made his first trip to Kansas City, Schlitz asked me to pick him up at the hotel and bring him to the brewery for their first meeting with him. Schlitz already had the broadcast contract but wanted to get to know him because they would be bidding for the rights in the future. In 1960 Schlitz had paid $400,000 for the broadcasts. Can you imagine that? Today they cost millions.

Anyway, I did pick him up. He sat in the back seat, as though I were his chauffeur. We went to the brewery where the meeting went fairly well. But on the way back to the hotel, all he could do was talk about moving the club out of Kansas City. That was the first hint I had of future trouble. Until that point, that subject had never come up. I knew I had become privy to something and I knew I had to keep quiet about it.

The only city that was mentioned that day was Dallas, but mostly it was moving anywhere. He was very much against Kansas City from the start, and I don't think from the moment he started negotiating with Carmen he ever had any intention of keeping the club in KC.

As soon as Finley bought the team, he started changing things. He brought in Frank Lane as general manager. Park Carroll still had a two-year contract that he had signed with Johnson, so when Finley brought in Lane, he refused to honor the contract and told Park to get his stuff out of the stadium. From that incident on it was clear that Finley's style was to demean and intimidate people.

Shortly afterwards, Park died of a heart attack. Finley's antics, I believe, were a major contributing factor.

The manager, Hank Bauer, was a victim of it too, and he left after Finley's first season. Finley hired Joe Gordon.

What was so distressing, though, was that people in Kansas City believed in Finley at first. He had everyone fooled. He would go around the city to make speeches but never hint that he was going to move the club. He still wanted revenue from attendance until he made the big announcement. I was feeling very uneasy about the future because you could see all he cared about was controlling people and situations.

People in town were getting excited about the A's though, because Finley was talking about all this innovation at the stadium and making it more of an entertainment value when they went to the ball park. He was talking about Harvey the Rabbit, a mechanical device that would deliver the baseball to the ump behind the plate. He came up with Charlie O., a mule mascot. He wanted sheep eating the grass behind the outfield fences. He talked about orange baseballs and brightly colored uniforms. But in truth, Finley was two-faced during this time and was hyping stuff as he worked behind the scenes to move the franchise where he felt he could create more attendance.

Of course, a contract with the city wouldn't allow him to move the team right away. At the end of the 1960 season, he personally approved the contracts for Merle and me to return for the 1961 season.

The off season was very much like the ones before, doing a lot of promotional work and preparing to go to spring training in West Palm Beach where the A's played their games at Connie Mack

At the A's spring training with Joe Gordon.

Stadium. Our first game that spring was March 11 against the Los Angeles Dodgers at Vero Beach. For Merle and me it was the beginning of the end as the A's broadcasters.

We stayed at the George Washington Hotel in West Palm Beach, and early on that spring we got yet another indication of Finley's nature. We were all in the bar one evening. Finley, Joe McGuff and Joe's boss at the Star, Ernie Mehl and me. We were all having a few beers. Swift, the third base coach, was also around somewhere. When Finley got a glimpse of him, he called him over and told him to get manager Joe Gordon down from his room to talk about the players.

"But Mr. Finley, Joe doesn't like to talk about players in a bar setting," he said to Finley. "It would be better to talk to him sometime tomorrow at the park."

"Look," Finley snapped back, "if you don't have the guts to call him, I'll do it myself!"

"Mr. Finley, Joe just doesn't like to be disturbed."

As it turned out, Finley called up to Gordon's room.

"Get your ass down here now!" Finley barked at him over the bar telephone. "Or I'm going to fire you."

About five minutes later, here comes Joe storming into the bar in his stocking feet and a tee shirt. He goes right up to Finley and grabs him by the throat and pulls him out of the chair.

"Look, you sonofabitch," Gordon begins, "I work for you, but you don't own me! If you want to fire me, fire me and give me my $25,000 right now."

Finley is choking at this point, and we're all sitting there stunned and wondering what was going to happen next.

"Uh...uh...I love a fighter, Joe," Finley was able to cough out. "You're my kind of manager. OK, let's talk about everything tomorrow at the ball park."

They shook hands, but everybody at that table knew that the Finley-Gordon relationship wasn't going to last.

Finley was amazingly naïve about how things worked in major league baseball, or how you went about things. After all, he had a mule for a mascot, goats grazing in the outfield and rabbits delivering balls to the umpire.

One night in New York, we were sitting in the bar again, this time with Gordon. I started pulling Finley's leg, but he never got it. I told him as long as he was going to have a mechanical rabbit coming up at home plate, why not have a similar gadget at the pitcher's mound and every time he wanted to change pitchers, just have them pop out of the ground right there at the mound.

Gordon kept kicking my leg trying to get me to stop. Except that Finley loved the idea and kept wanting more details from me on how it could be done.

Another time in the Big Apple, Finley called a news conference and got the entire New York media to come. The news guys were totally expecting something big. When they got there, Finley told them he had called the news conference to give one of the A's players, pitcher Ed Rocko, a nickname. From henceforth, Ed would be known as the Rocket. The press lambasted Finley for that one.

And Ed lived up to his nickname all right. Every time he went to the mound, they hit rockets off him.

Finley was fond of calling press conferences. Once in Chicago, Charlie called Hank Bauer late at night and told him to stick around the hotel in the morning because he was coming over. In the meantime, Finley had called a press conference for 11 o'clock. Bauer got wind of it, and knew it was to announce his firing as manager. So what did Hank do? He called a news conference for 10 and announced that he was quitting, just to upstage Finley. In all, Finley hired and fired Bauer three times.

But Finley was his own worst enemy. After the team had broken camp in 1961 and come north to Baltimore for the regular-season opener, he showed just how cheap he could be.

When we got to Maryland, the temperature was freezing. Frank Lane noticed that there was a men's store just across the street from the team hotel. As general manager he told his players to go across the street, pick out a hat to wear and the club would take care of the bill. Most everyone took advantage of Lane's generosity. When the final bill was tallied, it was about $700. But when Finley got word of the purchase he went into a tantrum and threatened to take it out of Lane's salary.

When I got wind of the incident, I called Charlie and told him what a brilliant public relations coup he had pulled off by suggesting to Lane that the team buy the players hats to warm their heads in the cold Baltimore air. I told him the gesture was making headlines all over the country.

"The Owner of the Kansas City A's is a Hero to his Team."

Finley paused, and then reconsidered his tirade against Lane, who never heard another word from his owner about the hats. Finley never knew he had been had.

I never had a confrontation with the man, but that's because I avoided it at all costs. Finley used to call me quite a bit and ask me to promote this or that on the radio. But he tried to use everybody, not just me. A lot of times when he couldn't get hold of Joe Gordon, Frank Lane, or Hank Bauer, he would call me. He believed me to be a weak sister. But he was wrong. I was determined to keep my job, but determined that I would never compromise my principles, either.

Finley was never hesitant to ruin a person if it would benefit Charlie O. He signed a pitcher by the name Lew Krause out of high school and paid him big bucks at the time, something like $40,000, which got big headlines. He then got the crazy idea of having him pitch the opener of a home series after we got back from the road in Minneapolis.

Gordon was absolutely against it, claiming that it would ruin the kid to throw him into the fire so early. Charlie really didn't care about that, and he figured it would draw a huge crowd and he could make back the $40,000 in a single game. As it turned out, Krause pitched a hell of a game, winning with a three-hitter and it made Charlie look like a genius. That first major league game that he pitched turned out to be one of the best of his career.

Finley always thought he could manipulate things with either money or by getting people beholden to him in other ways. He had to control people.

One year at spring training we had a media dinner and afterwards he tried to give everybody an expensive radio. He wasn't doing it out of the kindness of his heart; he wanted members of the media to be beholden to him. It was an awkward moment, but nobody wants to hurt another person's feelings by turning down a gift. Joe McGuff, the baseball beat writer for *The Star*, and Ernie Mehl, the sports editor, didn't understand Finley probably as well as Merle and I did.

We didn't want anything to do with the radio because we knew that Finley would eventually throw it up in our face. Poor Joe and Ernie took the radios, and it wasn't long before each wished he hadn't. That's probably because neither one of those guys was raised in a pool hall.

Eventually, Joe and Ernie started talking about Finley's desire to move the team from Kansas City. Charlie didn't like it, couldn't tolerate any adverse news that might affect attendance at the stadium. Finley, of course, talked to them about not writing about a possible move. But neither would agree to stop reporting the possibility, especially since it was now beginning to draw criticism from the public. When Finley realized he couldn't convince *The Star* guys from talking about the team moving out of Kansas City, he got real nasty. That's when he threw the gifts he had given them down in Florida in their face, claiming they shouldn't be giving Finley negative press since he had such a benefactor with the radios.

Of course, that just hardened Joe and Ernie's determination to report objectively what was happening with the A's and how Finley really planned to move them from the city all along. It got ugly, especially when McGuff and Mehl took the radios back to Finley and dumped them in his office.

Finley then tried to portray Mehl as a sportswriter who used a poison pen, mocking and making fun of Ernie. Finley went so far as to bring in a float before a game that mocked Ernie in front of the crowd. He even came to Merle and me to get us to make fun and ridicule Joe and Ernie to the radio audience. Neither Merle nor I would have anything to do with the scheme and, in no uncertain terms, we told him to bug out.

That did not sit well with Finley that we had sided with Joe and Ernie. He warned us that if we didn't talk about Joe and Ernie we might not be broadcasting the A's the following year. We even had other people from the front office come and urge us to give in to Finley's vendetta. They warned us that Finley would follow through on his threat.

Again we refused to trash our friends, not just because they were friends but because it was ethically and morally wrong, especially since we had direct knowledge that Finley would, in fact, move the team out of Kansas City as soon as his lease was up with the city.

We knew that we were finished with the A's that Finley would probably bring in Monte Moore to do the play-by-play the following year.

We ended up following Bauer's lead and quit before Finley could showboat at a news conference. Shortly afterwards, Finley hired Monte Moore. And when the team's lease with Kansas City expired after the 1966 season, Finley and Moore fled to the East Bay in Oakland, California, where eventually the Athletics won several World Series Championships.

There is no truth to the rumor, though, that every time I pass through Muncie, Indiana, I stop at the cemetery to relieve myself on Finley's grave. I did not hate Charlie Finley. I hated the way he carried himself and the way he did business.

It is extremely important that when you get out of bed every day that you truly enjoy what you do for a living and go about it with grace and humility. With Finley that wouldn't have been possible. I'm no Holy Joe, but I do have a conscience and a standard of ethics.

Charlie Finley could not say that.

My association with the A's ended when Merle and I broadcast our final game together on October 1, 1961, when the A's played a day game at Municipal Stadium against the Washington Senators.

The next time I would call a major league baseball game was 12 years later. By special request, Buddy Blattner and I broadcast the first game ever in Kauffman Stadium on April 10, 1973, between the Royals and Texas Rangers. Buddy and I did it for television since Denny Mathews was committed to the radio broadcast.

Blattner is in the same category with Merle and me. All of us started our broadcasting careers long before most of today's play-by-play men were even born.

"We were all workalcholics back then," said Buddy. "But Grigs especially so. You could call on Bill to do anything for you...or if you needed a speaker...and he would come on the twitch of a syllable. We were good friends back then but hadn't really worked together at all."

Ewing Kauffman had asked me personally to do it as a favor to him and the loyal baseball fans of Kansas City. How could I turn him...or myself...down with such an honor?

Of course I did the game with Buddy.

"We had a terrific time," Buddy said, "but then again Bill Grigsby is the type of guy who could find fun in a rainstorm at a ball game."

That day, though, was a beautiful day with no rainstorms...or mules, mechanical rabbits behind home plate or grazing goats in the outfield.

CHAPTER 7

Schlitz

I suppose you could say that Charlie Finley drove me to the bottle.

Literally.

Had it not been for the A's owner driving me out of major league baseball, I never would have become a beer wholesaler. Schlitz is the beer that made Milwaukee famous, but it was also the beer that led me to the modest financial independence that I enjoy today.

After Merle and I knew we weren't going to be returning as the A's broadcasters, it meant that we had to have a come-to-Jesus reckoning about our future. Walking away from a major league baseball job was difficult for both of us to accept. I don't think Merle was able to do it, but it was harder for me to walk away from what had become my home of Kansas City. Fran and I had established our family here, and we simply didn't want to leave.

Merle had the opportunity and took it to get back into baseball broadcasting. I had an opportunity to go to the Chicago White Sox, and also an audition with the Baltimore Orioles.

But it was really hard to come to that conclusion that this was pretty much the end of the baseball line for me, in that I had worked so hard to get to the major league level with the Athletics, and my style had improved so much I believed in the couple of years I did the games. It was disappointing and discouraging, even though I had been the one to choose to walk away.

Neither Merle nor I had been fired by Finley, but we probably would have been at some time in the future, because neither one of us would have been able to stomach some of the things he would have insisted from us.

I had enjoyed an excellent relationship with one of the main sponsors of the broadcast, the Schlitz Brewing Company, and with Guy Patterson of the Majestic Advertising Agency, the ad agency for the brewery.

One day after the word got out that Merle and I were done with Finley and the A's, I got a call from Hank DeBoer, who was running the Schlitz brewery in Kansas City.

"Bill, we want to talk to you. Can you come over?" he asked.

I had no idea what was up. When I got there, Hank explained that Schlitz had a small wholesaler business opening up north of the river in Kansas City and the company was interested in me taking it over. Hank said the Schlitz people had always been pleased with the way I handled the sponsorship on the game broadcasts. This would be a reward of sorts for my loyalty by bringing me into the business family.

Needless to say, I was overjoyed with the opportunity. I asked them how much money it would take on my part.

"About $80,000," was the reply.

"How much time do I have to raise the money?" I asked.

"Until tomorrow."

This was 1961 and I about swallowed by tongue. I didn't have that kind of money. I was living on a salary, living from week to week…from month to month, paycheck to paycheck.

But I never gave them any indication that I couldn't come up with the money, or that I wasn't interested. I just told them I would get back to them as quickly as I could.

I went downstairs to a pay phone and put in a call to a man named L.G. Skidmore.

Sometime in the late 1950s or the early 60s, I had spoken at a luncheon to some civic group. I guess I had done okay, because afterwards several people came up to me and told me how much they had enjoyed my talk. I recall this particular luncheon because a man identifying himself as L.Q. Skidmore had approached me and indicated that he had done well in business and appreciated my positive attitude that day.

He told me, almost in passing, that if I ever needed help in some way, to give him a call. It was as simple as that. But I never forgot the comment, because he had seemed so sincere and willing.

I guess it was nuts to some degree to believe I could call this Mr. Skidmore completely out of the blue and he would recall his offer several years removed from that luncheon. But crazy or not, that is exactly what I did.

It was a gruff but successful oilman who came to the line after I asked for Mr. Skidmore.

"Mr. Skidmore, this is Bill Grigsby," he began. "I met you a couple years ago after a luncheon."

"Yes, I remember," he said.

"Well, sir, at the time you complimented me by telling me you admired my outlook and you believed me to be a hard worker. You said if I ever needed help in business to call you. Well, sir, this is that call."

"Son, what is it you need?"

"Mr. Skidmore, I need $80,000 by tomorrow morning."

This is exactly the way I approached him, not trying to ease into the question. I was desperate. It was survival. There were five children at home. What was I going to do, ask him for a couple hundred bucks? I don't think so.

There was only a slight pause between my question and his answer.

"Meet me at my lawyer's tomorrow morning," he said.

It was just exactly and as straightforward as I describe it.

And the next morning a very happy 39-year-old Bill Grigsby went to R. Tucker's office at the firm of Tucker and Gage.

When I first laid it out, one of the lawyers told Mr. Skidmore he should not get into the beer business.

"I don't want to be the one who gets into the beer business," he responded in his gruff sort of way. "I want to help this young man get into the beer business."

That was pretty much all the lawyers had to say, and we drew up a five-year contract that would allow me to repay the loan. At the end of five years, I would own half the wholesaler and Mr. Skidmore the other 50 percent.

From there we walked down to Trader's Bank, L.Q. where I. Bob Dominick was the chairman of the board and Ray Evans the president.

"Give this man $80,000 and I'll sign a personal guarantee for it," he said flat out.

A short time later I signed some more papers. That was on October 27, 1961. I had bought a Schlitz wholesaler that quickly. And did I mention I had never seen it one time? The only thing I really knew was that it was located in Excelsior Springs, Missouri. And the only time I had ever been to Excelsior was to speak at a wild game banquet.

As anyone would be, I was excited about the next step in life. I knew it would be a challenge, and one completely different than I had taken on before. The first time I went to see what I had bought, it was hard to describe the feeling in the pit of my stomach.

The warehouse itself was only big enough to accommodate 5,000 cases of beer. Maybe. Then there was the floor caving in all the time and the holes in the walls where the drunks would sneak in and steal six-packs of beer.

Did I mention we were on the wrong side of the tracks of Excelsior?

Of course, it was a building that was impossible to heat in the winter and cool in the summer. I was lucky because the people who had worked for the previous owner agreed to stay on and work for me. Who could work in those kinds of conditions?

I hired a man to be my bookkeeper by the name of Mr. Finley High. The guy lived in south Kansas City and would drive 50 miles every day to work for me in Excelsior. I think he agreed to do that because he heard some of my broadcasts. Mr. High was the only man who knew how to get into the safe. It was a monster of a safe that looked like it would hold $80 million. The only money I think we ever kept in there, though, was a roll of nickels. Somebody tried to break into once and never did succeed. It's probably a good thing, because he would have been so mad at working so hard for nothing that he would have tracked me down and killed me.

What the whole thing boiled down to was trying to succeed in business without knowing a damn thing. I made a solemn vow, though, that after Mr. Skidmore had loaned me the money, I was somehow going to make it work...if not for me, for him at least. He was never involved in the business, never wanted to be. Once, however, he came up to Excelsior to say hi. I'll never forget his words to me after he saw it for the first time.

"Holy Mother of Jesus this is it?"

The first year of the business, the most I could pay myself in salary was $10,000. Obviously, I still had to do all my other free-lance stuff just to make ends meet. The business itself only made a profit of $1,200, but at least all of my employees had gotten paid.

Fran, meanwhile, prayed a lot that it wouldn't get too cold in the building and all the beer would freeze.

I actually did everything while I owned the business. Everything from calling on bar owners trying to get them to buy more Schlitz, to actually driving the trucks to deliver the beer. I usually got a pretty good reception from the bar people because most people in the area knew me from broadcasting.

I had inherited three trucks and a transport device that was in pretty poor shape. The beer transport was like an old horse that sagged in the middle. The day that it finally collapsed I sat and cried all day. Some guy in Parsons, Kansas heard about my plight and agreed to sell me a trailer in payments, otherwise I would have really been in a pickle. I also had a station wagon and would haul beer kegs around in that.

But even taking these kinds of measures wasn't working. The business wasn't making enough money for me to be able to even come close to paying back Mr. Skidmore. Finally, I figured out I was going to have to let one of my drivers go, and I would replace him on the route. I hated to do that, but there wasn't any other choice.

I brought all the guys together to tell them what had to be done. Basically, it came down to the last one hired under the old ownership, which was the youngest of the drivers.

"What route do you drive?" I asked him.

"The keg route."

I had no idea what that route was, or what it meant. I would later discover that it involved four counties—Clay, Platte, Ray and Clinton—and meant moving 300-pound kegs with no helpers. I worked the truck, got up early in the morning, loaded the 300-pound kegs and headed out to Liberty, Platte City, Plattsburg or wherever. I'd roll them up to the door and roll the empties back in the truck. Remember, at this point, I had never even driven a truck, much less lifted anything larger than a typewriter before.

I recall one place in Liberty called Shelby's. It had four steps up and the trick would be to get the truck positioned so I could at least unload the kegs at the steps. Every time I delivered to Shelby's I'd roll the keg off the back of the truck and when it hit the street, the people in the nearby businesses would come out to see what had happened. It never failed to draw people when I arrived. I believe some thought it might be an earthquake.

All the town drunks would come out and watch to see if I was going to make it up those steps. They were hopeful that I wouldn't and ask them to help me. They figured I'd give them a free beer. Of course, I couldn't afford to do that very often.

Once, one of the kegs got away from me and it was like the running of the bulls in Pamplona, Spain. What a sight it must have been for the town watching me chase that 300-pound keg down the streets of Liberty. I was just praying it wouldn't hit a car or a little kid. It finally hit a telephone pole. I got a round of applause from several bystanders. It had traveled about 50 yards and it took me the rest of the afternoon to get it back up there to Shelby's.

I was constantly being asked why I, as a celebrity, had to drive the truck.

"Oh, it's because I want to. It's because my doctor advised me to be getting more exercise and this was a good way to do it," I told them.

Baloney.

But never once did I feel as though I was degrading myself by having to do this part of the work. I had never failed to answer the bell, even when I was cleaning puke out of the theater in Joplin. Somebody had to do it, and so what if I was the president of the corporation? I had to do it in order to make it. My ego wasn't going to get in the way.

Some days a driver wouldn't show up for work and I would have to do the keg route, hurry back and also do the bottle route. I did that once, but was in too much of a rush and ended up dumping 50 cases of beer out onto the highway.

When I took over, we were selling about 175,000 cases a year. But the margin on beer sales at that time was terrible. We got something like 10 cents a case, so you had to sell a lot of the stuff. In all of those four counties there were only a few big cities: North Kansas City, Excelsior Springs and Richmond.

And you couldn't raise the price because the market was so competitive. Our main competition was Falstaff, Ham's and Budweiser.

I learned the hard way about Falstaff on one trip to a customer in Richmond. I was hauling beer into a joint with a two-wheeler when I passed a couple guys at the bar. As I passed them, I was feeling good about the business and told the barkeep to give them a beer. When I finished and was coming back through, the bartender told me that would be $2.50. He had given them a Falstaff.

In addition to having to deliver beer, I also made sales calls hoping to pump up the business. That meant a lot of beer drinking with the customers, which meant that I would get half drunk by the time I got home at night. It got to be a vicious cycle, and there were times when I cried myself to sleep at night wondering what in the world I had gotten myself and family into.

I was still doing a lot of extra jobs on the side during this time, again, just to make ends meet. I was still refereeing on Friday and Saturday nights. So I was not spending a lot of quality time at home with my family. But then again I was keeping them fed and clothed.

I would work all day long delivering beer, then spend Friday nights running up and down a football field officiating a high school game.

One night I didn't get home until about 11 o'clock. When I walked into the door, Fran told me I had gotten a call from the police in Excelsior and that somebody had broken into the warehouse. So I jumped in the car, raced about 50 miles to the police station only to be told they couldn't spare me any men to go investigate. They handed me a flashlight and told me to go.

Of course, by the time I got there, nobody was around. This happened about five or six times while the warehouse was in Excelsior, and each time I wouldn't get back to bed until 4:30 in the morning.

But slowly things began to improve. Where once I had gone into a bar and seen a guy drinking Falstaff, I began to see more and more of those guys with a bottle of Schlitz in their hands. That was encouraging and kept me going psychologically. At least it gave me the ability to start dealing with some of the other small setbacks, like the raccoons falling through the ceiling and defecating all over my desk. We even had an office pot going on which ceiling square they would fall through. Pick the right square, and you'd win two dollars.

We had mice. They would come in because they liked the glue on the bottle labels. Then the mice attracted snakes. It was one big happy family of crooks, raccoons, mice and snakes.

The mice were probably the biggest problem, especially one year when the dark suits of the Internal Revenue Service came to visit. I had been in business about two years and had not made all that much money, when a car pulled up and these guys got out. I looked at Mr. High and said we were about to get audited. That is exactly what was happening.

I wasn't all that worried, because I hadn't really made a nickel in the business; I hadn't even been able to steal anything.

"This is Mr. High, he's my bookkeeper," I told the two men when they walked in. "And you can use my desk to do your work. I'll be out on the beer truck delivering."

"That's fine. Where's the coffee?" they asked.

I explained to them we didn't have any water coming into the place.

"But what about the toilet?"

"If I have to go, I go over to the Elms Hotel, and the drivers go up the street at the Texaco. Wanna beer?"

They weren't too humored.

About the only problem we really had with the IRS audit, though, was once we started going through the records, we noticed that the mice had eaten the records for October. As it turned out, we didn't owe anything and, in fact, they gave us some money back.

It wasn't until the fourth year that the business began to show some promise. We raised our prices. Our margin jumped up to 28 cents a case and we were able to increase our sales to about 200,000 cases a year. Nevertheless, I was still on the truck.

By the fifth year, I had paid back about half of what I owed Mr. Skidmore, but I still owed him $40,000 which I didn't have. I was worried sick that he might die and someone would call me on the note and all the hard work of the last five years would go for naught. I would have lost the business if anything had happened to Mr. Skidmore.

So I went to him again, explained my fears and offered him $20,000 now if he would give me control of the company.

Again, he was incredibly gracious and agreed.

We went to the bank to get him his money, but bank officials explained to me I didn't have enough equity in the business to do it. They told me I needed a co-signer and recommended someone who didn't give me a particularly good rate. Even still, I was amenable and did the deal.

When I went to Mr. Skidmore, though, he asked me where I had gotten the money and I explained the whole story. He became extremely agitated, not at me, but at the bank for putting me in that position.

But at least I had paid my debt to Mr. Skidmore, and that, believe me, took a lot of stress off me. He signed over the remaining 500 shares of the company to me on April 13, 1970. I still have the signed "Paid" receipt from Mr. Skidmore.

It was also about this time in 1968 when I decided to finally give up my referring that I had done for two decades. I wrote a letter on April 24, 1968, to Steve Connor, who was head of the officials, explaining my decision.

"This is a not an easy decision to make," I wrote.

"However, the press of business and limitations on my time available for family life, make it necessary. I have decided to hang them up. I finished 20 years with the 1967 season…and it has been most rewarding, particularly in the friendships that I have made.

"Thank you, Steve…and I guess I should send a thanks to Al Henshaw. He loaned me the first officiating garb I had in Kansas City, because I was too poor to buy it."

As things began to look up with my business and my family life, I moved the business from Excelsior to a warehouse in North Kansas City. That was in the seventh year.

We moved to a warehouse at 1540 Atlantic in 1968, and it was the first time since I had bought the business that my drivers and family members didn't have to work in freezing conditions during the winter. The only reason that the beer had never frozen in the Excelsior warehouse is because it was right next to the railroad tracks and the trains came by just often enough to shake the bottles and keep them from freezing.

But even though we had moved to much better quarters, that didn't mean there weren't problems on occasion.

By the early 1970s, the business began to do well. The hard work had paid off, and we were now delivering as many as 300,000 cases a year. I was still paying myself a bit more salary and the business was building up a good equity. It had become a very solid investment, and by the ninth year it had been paid off and was fully clear.

The kids were in college by that time, and I felt good about things because I was able to pay for that. It was also about this time we moved our household north of the river, which made it a lot easier for me to get to the warehouse in the morning. And every once in a while, Mr. Skidmore would come by in the morning to see how I was doing.

And then one day he died. He had been living in an apartment on the Plaza. By the time I got the word he had already been taken to a funeral home and cremated. That had been his wish.

I was the first one to be notified, because he had listed me as such. He had no other family and his wife had died earlier. I dearly loved the man and still pray for him every time I go to mass. I pray for his soul, because it was L.Q. Skidmore who made all the difference in my life.

Even in death, Mr. Skidmore had a few surprises for me. Several days after he died, I got a call from the First National Bank. When I went to the bank, I was told that Mr. Skidmore had bequeathed me $20,000! It was the $20,000 he had always felt bad about taking from me when I paid him off with the borrowed money. I cry a little even when I think about it today.

But by 1972 there were some things going on with Schlitz that I began to question, even though we were now selling about 450,000 cases a year. Things were going very well, but I had this underlying feeling that something wasn't right with Schlitz.

So on August 31, 1972, I made the decision to sell the business. I called and wrote Don Dahlgren of the company to inform him of my intentions.

"Dear Don,

"This letter will confirm our conversation of August 30 regarding the possibility of the sale of Bill Grigsby, Inc.

"At this time I wish to make known my desire to sell this Schlitz wholesalership, providing a buyer agrees to terms and has the approval of the Joseph Schlitz Brewing Co.

"Thank you."

A businessman by the name of Joe Brancato came forward to say he wanted to buy the business as it was flourishing and was No. 1 in the marketplace at this point. We were beating even Budweiser.

I took his offer home to Fran and we discussed in fully. She reminded me that it was I who had suddenly grown uncomfortable with the recent Schlitz management decisions.

"Go ahead and sell, Bill," she said.

I went to the Schlitz people and told them. They asked whom I was selling it to, and after I told them they indicated I couldn't sell it to Joe. There were others on a waiting list who wanted it. As it turned out, it went to a guy named Truman Sloan, much to Joe Brancato's dismay.

After the sale was completed, it enabled me to relax mentally. For the first time in my life I was not burdened by any kind of debt. Growing up I remembered what it had done to my mother always having to dodge the gas man. Overriding debt is what killed my mother and father, so it was like lifting a life-long burden for me to be in this situation. I was 51 years old and the years of driving a truck and struggling were now behind me. It was 1973, my house was paid for, and for the first time I didn't have a burden of worries. I didn't owe anyone any favors and wasn't beholden to anyone.

And it was very soon that even Brancato was happy that I kept him out of the deal. Shortly after I got out of the Schlitz business, the brewery made some awful management decisions and within two years the company went belly up. A 150-year old company had been busted by bad management choices, primarily by the decision to use synthetic hops.

I had been extremely lucky in life again. Had I hung on to the franchise I would have suffered total disaster, and my life would be very different today, perhaps.

Again, God had been looking down upon old Grigs. I believe as much.

Our money was safely in the bank, and we had been living in our new home on Crooked Road for just over a year, the kind of home Fran had wanted all her life. All our bills were paid and the Chiefs had become extremely popular in Kansas City.

I had lots of speaking engagements on my calendar, I was being courted as a PR man for Interstate Securities and there was talk of the city getting a new sports franchise, a hockey team that would compete in the National Hockey League.

I got a call from a man named Ed Thompson.

Life was good.

CHAPTER 8

The Scouts

I proudly wear the ring of a world champion on my right hand, a glitzy reminder of Super Bowl IV when the Chiefs dismantled the Minnesota Vikings. And since I had an opportunity to do a couple games with the Royals, I have also have the honor of being involved with Kansas City's other world champion.

But probably few realize that I was also on the ground floor of yet a third Kansas City franchise that went on to win a couple world championships, the Scouts.

Kansas City's entry into the National Hockey League came on June 8, 1972, when Edwin Thompson was awarded one of two expansion franchises. The other, the Capitals, went to Washington D.C.

Knowing my background in both the business and sports communities, Eddie called me shortly after I had sold my beer business. The timing couldn't have been better. I had a little money and was looking for a new but different kind of challenge.

The NHL had given Ed about two years to put a team on the ice with the first season scheduled for the fall of 1974. He wanted me to run the business side of the organization and had hired Sid Abel to administer the players' end of things. Sid had a long and highly regarded history in hockey and was a terrific choice to get the sport off to a flying start in Kansas City.

I also became a minority stockholder with a small $35,000 investment. There were numerous other smaller investors, including Hank Stram and Gene Novor, the owner of Michael's Clothier's.

One of our first orders of business was coming up with a name for the new team, a mascot that fans could quickly identify and bond with. Because of the Native American heritage of the area, we became the Scouts, and our logo was patterned after the bronze statue that sits atop Penn Valley Park. But few people know that it actually was our second choice for a mascot.

The first choice was Mo-Hawks. But the Chicago Black Hawks who, understandably, felt it was too closely related to their team mascot, vetoed it. We were able, however, to get the team colors that we wanted: Yellow, Blue, Red and White.

The only downside for me in getting involved with the Scouts was that it cut into my involvement with the Chiefs. I couldn't continue to be broadcasting Chiefs' games since I now was financially and emotionally occupied with another sports franchise. So after 11 years in the Chiefs broadcast booth, I had to take a leave of absence for what turned out to be a few years. I did not, however, give up my affiliation with Lamar's grand creation. I handled the stadium public address during my two-year exile.

Although Dick Carlson was hired to do the Scouts' play-by-play, I also was in the broadcast booth doing the color commentary and sometimes taking over for Dick in calling the action. It was a whole new experience for Dick and me since neither one of us had ever broadcast hockey, much less NHL hockey before.

Probably the job I enjoyed most during my hockey career was making sales calls in New York City with the Seagram's Company, distillers of a popular whiskey called VO. It was Sid's beverage of choice, and after he got me to try it, it became mine as well. So it was a labor of love working with Seagram's and trying to convince the company to plop down a half million bucks for a sponsorship that ultimately would be used to buy a scoreboard for Kemper.

I'll never forget the day I got back from New York after completing the deal. Eddie and I got together for a drink so I could bring him up to date on the sponsorship, and he was sitting at the bar drinking Canadian Club. I explained to him that that had to stop, that it was VO's main competitor. He resisted at first, but he eventually came around. Money has a tendency to change people's taste in whiskey sometimes. Eddie was a high roller. He liked to

Howdy Pardner! I love rodeo.

smoke the biggest Cuban cigars and stay in the biggest and best hotels when we went on the road. Today he lives in Arizona.

Sid had hired a top-notch coach in Bep Guidolin and there had been a great deal of hoopla over our first draft choice, Wilf Paiment, who was assigned the first ever Scouts jersey, No. 9.

Wilf was a highly regarded player who was able to live up to his billing. But he cost a lot of money to sign. Part of the deal also required us to bring in his parents to Kansas City from the Canada backwoods four times a year so they could see their son's games.

Sid had to go meet his parents once when we were in the process of trying to complete the deal with Paiment. Sid had quite a story when he got back to the office. Apparently his parents lived in a remote area and their house was on the side of a hill. All the exterior and interior doors didn't quite fit right, and since the house was on a tilt, none of them ever quite shut. And if you had to use the toilet in the bathroom, you had to devote one hand to holding the door shut, because it would simply swing open under normal circumstances.

And I guess Wilf's parents were quite a sight. They had never had a chance to spend much time in the big city. When they would come to our games here, everyone would wince. Wilf's dad might come dressed in yellow pants, a purple shirt and a green hat.

Wilf never turned out to be the marquee guy we had hoped, but he was a good, solid player. The trouble was, most of the other players around him were pretty much NHL re-treads whom we got in the expansion draft. Each team was able to protect 16 players, so those left were pretty much the scrubs.

There was a lot of excitement about the team in the early going, and we sold around 8,000 season tickets, which wasn't all that bad. Our first home game was November 2, 1974, against the Black Hawks, and we did attract 15,000 for that game.

Our very first game was October 9 in Toronto. We lost to the Maple Leafs, 6-2, then to the New York Islanders, 6-3, and then to the Flyers in Philadelphia 3-2. Our first encouraging sign came on October 23 in California when the Scouts tied the Seals 4-4.

We finished our first month 0-7-1.

Our first victory came in early November when we beat our expansion sisters, the Washington Capitals, 5-4.

When the damage was totaled up after the first season, the Scouts were 15-54-11, but at least we didn't have the worst record in the league. That belonged to the Capitals.

During that first season, a reporter asked Bep if it was a nightmare coaching such a hapless team. He gave them a great answer.

"You gotta be able to sleep before you have nightmares," he said.

There was one great moment in that first season, however. In what could only be described as one of the biggest upsets in NHL history, the Scouts did go into the Boston Gardens one evening and beat Phil Esposito, Bobby Orr and the Bruins, 3-2.

After that first season, I began to see holes in the organization. I became uncomfortable with 37 owners and some of the mismanagement caused by trying to appease such a large group. We had sold 8,000 season tickets that first season, but after a hard sell could only get about 2,000 going into the second year.

As far as I was concerned, it just wasn't working. I went to Eddie and told him I just didn't like the way he was letting everybody who owned a piece of the team have a say in how it was being run. It was a mess, so I pulled my money out after about a year.

Overall, the second year wasn't much better than the first. They won three fewer games and the most notable stat from that second season was the fact that one of the Scouts players, Steve Durbano, did go into the record books as having the most penalty minutes in the league. He had 370 minutes in the penalty box during the 1975-76 season.

What was sad about that second season is that there had been a lot of playoff talk, but that was impossible when the Scouts lost 27 straight games in one stretch. About halfway through, rumors began to grow that the team was going to move to Denver after only two seasons in Kansas City. That pretty much cooled any enthusiasm that we might have created the first couple of years.

By the end of the second year, the Scouts were nearly $1 million in debt and were headed to the Mile High City.

Towards the end, we had a visit from the Internal Revenue Service. The IRS wanted to talk to all the stockholders. When one young IRS woman talked to me, she questioned how much we paid the players, suggesting that it was too much.

"Let me tell you," I told her. "You are absolutely right. Those players that you've looked at? Well, they're not worth 50 cents apiece. I just did what everybody in the organization did, put down what we hoped they were worth. I went along with it."

The IRS eventually determined that we were writing off too much for the value of the players. In the end it cost everybody in the organization a little money that we had to pay back to the IRS.

I don't have any regrets about my involvement in the Scouts. Although it never worked out, it was fun. It was never funded in the way it should have been or what it would take by today's standards. In retrospect, it never had a chance, considering the components.

But I got to meet a lot of great folks that I normally wouldn't have, including athletes I had never been exposed to before. They were tough guys who had a funny way of talking because they were all from Canada. Most of them had been involved in hockey since they were five years old because that's the way it worked up north.

And I loved Sid Abel. We had some great times drinking Canadian whiskey and having some wild arguments. More than any league I've been associated with, they really know how to put away the booze in the National Hockey League.

One year I went to training camp up in Michigan to get to know the players better. Their routine is to work very hard during the day, party just as hard that night and then try to burn all the booze out in the morning in the sauna. Sounded like a great plan to me.

After a couple of days I got into the swing of things but sans the sauna. But after one particularly hard night, I was very much in need of a little hot steam, but I wasn't familiar with where the sauna was located. So from the second-floor locker room, with my little towel, I went in search of the sauna. I should have made sure I knew where I was headed.

I opened the door to what I thought was the sauna, but then the door shut behind me with a certain permanency and it was completely dark. I knew I was in trouble when I turned the doorknob and it was locked. I start pounding on the door, but nothing.

I finally decided to try to feel my way along the dark hallway. I went only a short distance before I felt a set of stairs, which I went down. After making my way down to what I believed to be the first floor, I saw a dim sliver of light surrounding a door. I headed that way, again completely naked except for my white towel.

Much to my delight, the door was open and I stormed through. I popped right to the outdoors and the door slammed right behind me, again locked against re-entry. So there I was standing out in front of a hotel in a Michigan college town with nothing but a small towel not much larger than a washcloth. I felt like a naked Peter Sellers creeping around in the movie *A Shot in the Dark*, trying to avoid detection and trying to remain nonchalant.

I had come out on the side of the building, and the only way back was through the front lobby of our hotel. The first person I encountered was a little old lady who was appalled at what she was seeing.

"Mornin' mum," I timidly said as she just scowled.

As I got to the lobby, I ran into Sid who couldn't quite believe what he was seeing. I told him I'd explain later as I dashed by, through the lobby and towards the elevators.

As it turned out, it was the highlight of camp for everybody.

That, as it turned out, was one of the *good* memories of being with the Scouts. Once I decided to leave, I quickly got a call from Paul Hamilton, who invited me to come to work at Interstate Securities, which was a loan company.

Meanwhile, the Scouts did, in fact, move to Denver and became the Colorado Rockies. They stayed there until 1982 and didn't enjoy much more success than during the two years they were in Kansas City. The loss of hockey in Kansas City represented a major disappointment for the NHL, which had not lost an expansion franchise since the 1934 season when the team in Ottawa left to go to St. Louis.

But the Scouts' exit wasn't the only switch that season. The Seals also pulled out of California and headed to Cleveland as the Barons.

The Rockies' only claim to fame was that the team did make the playoffs several years after leaving Kansas City. But again after a change of ownership, the franchise finally made it big in New Jersey, attracting big crowds and winning the Stanley Cup championship in 1995, 2000 and 2003.

I followed the team only slightly after they left for Colorado and probably even less once they got to New Jersey. But Fran and I did bet on them last year when they got to the Stanley Cup finals against the Anaheim Mighty Ducks. I bet on the Ducks, Fran on the Scouts...uh, Devils.

Today, the Devils are owned by a group headed up by George Steinbrenner. A far cry from Eddie Thompson, Hank Stram and Bill Grigsby.

CHAPTER 9

The Chiefs' Early Years

Who could have predicted that when a young Texas businessman came to Kansas City in the early 1960s that it would mean so much to the future of the community and to my own life.

Certainly, there was nothing in his soft-spoken and quiet demeanor that suggested that the 26-year-old Lamar Hunt would have such a profound impact. At the very least, he was a breath of fresh air after having to deal with Charlie Finley for so long.

The Chiefs, of course, are the centerpiece of Lamar's endeavors here for the past four decades. But he has brought so much more in the form of neighborhood development, international trade, the soccer Wizards, and for a few years, world championship tennis.

And he was responsible for helping make Kansas City a major summer tourist destination by building Worlds of Fun and Oceans of Fun. He no longer owns either, but the two amusement parks remain a summer cornerstone of family activity.

Lamar first came to Kansas City in the winter of 1962, just after his Dallas Texans had won the American Football League Championship in a memorable game against the Houston Oilers.

The mayor, H. Roe Bartle, coaxed Lamar to town at the time. Roe and I were good friends, and he kept insisting that he believed there was a good chance Kansas City could get Lamar to move the team here because Hunt was having problems with the city of Dallas in its support of the Texans.

When Lamar came to town to develop a business plan in moving his team to Kansas City, Mayor Bartle asked me if I would show him around. He asked if I would take him to Excelsior Springs, introduce him around and let him get to know the kind of people who lived in this area. H. Roe wanted me to escort him around Excelsior because he knew that's where my Schlitz warehouse was located and that I had a lot of contacts up there. Lamar was going to be speaking to a civic group that night and hopefully convince some people to purchase season tickets. He did sell some, but it wasn't an easy sell.

Lamar had already decided to move the team here, but going to Excelsior, I think, was designed to help solidify that decision in his own mind. On the way up in the car, I told him I would personally buy eight season tickets. But despite that gesture, I was technically only the 13th person to first purchase Chiefs season tickets. And, of course, I am still a season ticket holder. Back then a season ticket cost $49, or seven dollars a game.

When the team moved here from Dallas, the name was changed from the Texans to the Chiefs, in large measure because of H. Roe Bartle. Bartle was known as the "Chief" for his keen political savvy and for his work with the Boy Scouts.

Later on, the Chiefs came to Merle and me to ask if we would radio broadcast the Chiefs' football games. Lamar knew we had done the baseball A's but had had a falling out with Charlie Finley and were available. Needless to say, both Merle and I were delighted to be back involved in professional sports, although we had done some college football games. We did the Chiefs' first year before Merle went on to New York to do the Jets' games and the Milwaukee Braves in baseball during the summer.

After Merle left, Tom Hedrick joined me in the second year of the Chiefs' broadcasts. Tom was also doing the University of Kansas play-by-play. Tom and I worked well together, although he had a reputation of being a motormouth. He was always talking.

This was 1963 and doing college games was probably as big, if not bigger, than doing the AFL. But even in their first year, the Chiefs had a pretty good radio network on KCMO-AM. Schlitz and Interstate Securities Company were the anchor sponsors.

This has always been a great football market, with Missouri, Kansas and Kansas State in this area. But there was some skepticism about the AFL when it first arrived. The people were not all that familiar with the players, and the first game, which was against Buffalo, drew only about 5,000 fans. Even for a preseason game, that was pretty frightening. After that, though, I think it started picking up pretty fast.

People here were very much aware of the AFL-NFL battle and the competition for players. I think the big question in everybody's

Early pioneers of the AFL, from left: me, Len Dawson, Lamar Hunt and NBC's Charlie Jones.

mind was whether the AFL owners had enough money to outlast the NFL. Even then, Lamar called himself and the other AFL team owners the members of The Foolish Club, for their insistence that they could buck the NFL giant. But if you looked at them, they were all pretty strong, with Lamar and Bud Adams of the Houston Oilers certainly the strongest members of the original group. It was Wayne Valley of the Oakland Raiders who actually came up with the name The Foolish Club. Wayne was one of the initial owners of the Raiders, obviously before the arrival and invention of Al Davis.

It was well documented in the early going of the AFL that Lamar was losing a million dollars a year on the Texans and Chiefs. A business reporter asked Lamar's father, H.L. Hunt, if that was prudent business and how long Lamar could do it.

"Oh, maybe 150 years," H.L. said sarcastically.

H.L. Hunt amassed his wealth in Texas oil and was well known long before his son invented the AFL. I met him once while I was visiting Lamar at his home in Dallas. H.L. was living with Lamar, and while I was there at the house, the telephone rang and H.L. asked me to answer it. Lawrence Welk was on the line and hoping to talk to H.L., who didn't want to talk and asked me to tell him to call back some other time.

It was that kind of world Lamar had grown up in, so creating the AFL maybe wasn't all that big a deal after all.

Actually, the only weak AFL link was Harry Wismer, owner of the New York Titans, who later became the Jets. When payday rolled around in the Titans' camp, the practice session would always end right then and there so the players could run to the bank to get their checks cashed.

Sonny Werblin would eventually buy the team and was one of the straws that broke the NFL's back. Sonny was not afraid to spend money, and one of the most important checks he wrote was to sign Joe Namath for an unheard of $400,000. Of course, by today's standards that is nothing, but back then it meant the AFL was playing for keeps.

But when Lamar came to Kansas City, I think the town needed something to get recharged. There was a lot of controversy about Finley, who was constantly talking about moving the A's. In a way, I think that's why the momentum for the Chiefs began to pick up, because everybody was so fed up with the A's situation.

There weren't too many memorable moments in the early going for the Chiefs. Probably the most noteworthy was the preseason game played in Wichita when Stone Johnson was hurt and later died. That was a very tragic and awful beginning for this franchise.

And the team played in some very shabby and unusual places in the early days. In Boston, I remember a game in the Harbor Stadium once. We played the Raiders in Portland, Oregon, in an old baseball stadium. Sometimes there would only be two shower stalls for the players and they had to take turns. I think it was a case of a lot of people just not believing the league was going to be around for very long, so why bother.

Of course, the Chiefs when they played at home in Kansas City, were playing in an old baseball stadium, Municipal Stadium. That is where the A's played, and as it turned out it was also a pretty good football stadium. Then when the Chiefs started doing well and drawing crowds of 50,000, they added the temporary stands on the side.

When I see old films of games there, I see the great big billboard, "When you're out of Schlitz you're out of beer!" That gives me warm and fuzzy feelings since Schlitz was a major sponsor and I was the distributor for part of the area.

In fact, it was getting involved in the beer business that kept me from pursuing other baseball broadcast deals like Merle had gotten in Milwaukee. I knew that's what he wanted and wasn't surprised when he left after only one year. I had decided not to leave because Fran and I liked it here so much.

Lamar and the AFL enjoyed some big victories over the NFL in the early going but also suffered some painful setbacks. One of the most striking for Lamar was Minnesota being lured away from AFL into the NFL. Max Winter and a group of Minneapolis and

St. Paul businessmen were committed to Lamar, but at the last second went with the older league. It was very much a bitter pill for Lamar and very much on his mind when the Chiefs played the Vikings in Super Bowl IV in New Orleans on January 11, 1970.

The night before the game, Fran and I, along with Lamar and Norma, Joe McGuff and his wife, Kay, were having dinner at Antoine's. Although the French Quarter is raucous, Antoine's is sedate. We were sitting in the 1849 Room, and Lamar started pounding the table and chanting, "KILL, KILL, KILL."

Everybody in the 1849 Room looked around at the seemingly mild-mannered man who had been transformed into the Incredible Hulk. It had everything to do with playing the Vikings, the traitors. I am not sure he still doesn't harbor bad feelings toward the franchise.

Even though Lamar was a young man when he brought Kansas City a pro football franchise, no one seemed to question his age. His background and experience seemed to trump the fact that he was still under 30. Besides, everybody quickly became impressed with his moneyman, Jack Steadman, an impressive guy in both physical stature and class. It tells you a lot about both Lamar and Jack that they have been together as friends and businessmen since 1958. It is a tribute to what true loyalty is all about, whatever you think of either one of them.

Then there was The Mentor.

Hank Stram is one of the most memorable men I have ever met. He was a Notre Dame assistant who was so excited to get his chance in pro football. And as history tells us, one of the most innovative minds the game has known. He had inventive defensive alignments, rolling pockets on offense. And although he won that championship game against Houston as the Texans' coach, the most games the Chiefs won the first three years they were in Kansas City was seven. He got a lot of criticism from around the league because everybody believed the team was loaded with talent and the only thing holding it back was the coach.

Hank eventually had the last laugh by taking the Chiefs to the first Super Bowl in Los Angeles and later to the one in New Orleans.

There was a close fraternity back in the early days of the franchise. Hank was very loyal to his coaches, people like Tom Pratt, Pete Brewster, Bill Walsh, Tom Bettis. Hank was very appearance conscience and strict. He had strict dress codes and would have his assistants administer tests to the players on road trips.

The entourage also included Wayne Rudy, the trainer, and Bobby Yarborough, the equipment manager. The players absolutely loved Wayne, who had a quiet personality in much the same way as Lamar did. Bobby was the opposite, and at times cantankerous. But everybody got along, maybe because nobody back then was making a whole lot of money, including the players.

Players would make about $8,000, or about $700 a game. Of course, that didn't stop anybody from playing card games during our road trips. We played booray for money, and Sherrill Headrick would sometimes lose his whole paycheck on the way to the game. Booray is a card game played mostly in the south, particularly in Cajun country. It is similar to spades. The ante is small, but the pots can grow quickly as Sherrill found out.

I remember when we were first traveling how much different it was than today. We would take the team bus to the airport, but instead of going directly to a chartered airplane like today, we would actually stop in front of the terminal and walk through the airport and through the gate just like everybody does. And there were times when players, who might be a little beat up from practice, would stop off at the airport bar and slam down a few shots of whiskey before even getting on the plane to make themselves feel better.

Most of the players were aware I was also in the beer business in the early days of the Chiefs, and some players, most notably Headrick, had a standing order for ten cases of Schlitz waiting for him when we came home from a road trip. The first thing we would do when we got back was to go to my car and make the switch to his.

Sherrill was a one-of-a-kind athlete, a throwback. One week, after hemorrhoid surgery, we were on a flight for a road game, and when the airplane left, Sherrill was sitting on one of those inflatable donuts. But about halfway through the trip, once the Schlitz kicked in, the donut ended up around his head.

Eventually, we would pass out two cans of Schlitz to each player when they got on the plane after the game for the trip home. Some of the players, though, had a little bit more of an edge so they might need more beer. We generally would put a whole case in the seats of Ed Budde, Fred Arbanas and Sherrill. Some of the players could swallow a case of beer in no time. Especially after a warm day in San Diego.

There is a certain image of Hank Stram today that does not necessarily fit with who Hank was when he first came to Kansas City from Texas with Lamar. He did not have the larger-than-life persona and big ego that some associate with him after he and the Chiefs started getting a lot of national attention.

In the early years, he was just another guy trying to make it in the world. He and I would sometimes go out after practice and kick a football around. We would bet on kicking field goals out at the team's original practice facility on 63rd Street in Swope Park. On the road, we would often pitch quarters, or if there was a ping-pong table we would play that. Hank loved that kind of thing, the friendly competition.

Later, he would goad the players into taking him on. One time he was playing table tennis with running back Mike Garrett. The two of them got into a big argument when Hank intentional-ly hit the ball into a wall next to the table and it came down on Garrett's side. Mike argued that the ball had gone out, and it was his point. Hank didn't see it that way, of course, and tried to con-vince everyone that his tactic was legal. Mike became extremely agitated with his coach because of that incident.

That is sort of the way Hank played golf, but we never called it cheating. To Hank, a ball never got lost, went out of bounds or was in the rough. We wouldn't accuse him of cheating, only using magic balls.

It was the same in racquetball, only then he would hit the ball into the backs of players, and then try to claim that it was his point.

The truth is that Henry was born with a competitive instinct, whether it was for football or pitching quarters.

I remember one game in St. Louis when guard George Daney got ejected from a game for hitting someone with his fist. Daney was banished to the locker room, but Hank simply waited about 15 minutes and put somebody else's uniform on him and brought him back into the game. The officials were not idiots, though. They knew immediately what was going on and Hank later got fined for that little stunt.

That was Hank Stram.

Hank, during his tenure, also got lots of gifts. He would use the ones he was happy to get. The ones he didn't particularly care for, he would store away in a closet. Then every year when it got to be around Christmas, he would give them to us in the Chiefs' traveling party. Of course, he would try to tell us that he had gone out and picked them specifically for whomever he was giving it to. But we all knew the truth about what was happening.

Clothes were also very important to Hank. You see some people today on corners with signs reading: "Will work for food." Well, if need be, Hank would have stood on a corner with a sign that read, "Will work for clothes."

Hank had an arrangement with a guy who made custom clothes. Hank would get custom duds in exchange for doing his commercials. Hank drove the guy nuts. He ended up with so many suits he ran out of closet space and made the guy start making clothes for his kids.

Hank's wife, Phyllis, was a settling influence on the man. She was the only one, maybe, who was able to control and keep Hank anchored on this earth.

Don't get me wrong about Hank, though. He was a man and a coach who brought a winner to Kansas City. Hank Stram is a winner, even though it's delightful to poke a little fun at his eccentricities. Hank and I are very much on the same page when it comes to what it takes to be a success: ACE.

Vitamins? Not exactly.

A is for attitude, baby. My life is a lot like a prizefight. There are going to be a lot of rounds and I'm going to get knocked down a time or two. The key is to be ready for the next round. That's attitude.

C? That's communication. You're only going to go as far as your ability to communicate allows you to with other people.

And finally **E** is for enthusiasm. If you haven't gotten enthusiasm for the game of life, then forget it.

Hank had ACE, all of it. And that's what I preach to young people today.

He also was a great showman, obviously. He was very concerned about his image and how he came across in the newspapers, radio and on TV. He made the technique of wiring coaches during games popular. The classic is when he was wired for Super Bowl IV.

The networks had also done it for other games, and Hank never told the players that he had a microphone. But Lenny Dawson and some of the players could always tell when Hank was wired, because the coach would go into long and flowery explanations during the game and, according to Lenny, he never did that unless it was being recorded. Hank was playing to TV.

The war with the NFL was still going on, and it was only because of Lamar's patience and persistence that that AFL hung in there. Few know about it, but Lamar was always working behind the scenes in fighting the football war. One of his targets had been Roman Gabriel, the outstanding quarterback who eventually signed with the Los Angeles Rams. Lamar, though, came very close to signing him. Lamar had talked with him on the telephone for several hours about details of a contract. Years later, Lamar found out that he had not been talking to Gabriel, but Elroy Hirsch, the general manager of the Rams. It was classic of the AFL-NFL wars and indicative of the kind of atmosphere that existed between the two factions.

Of course there were victories as well. Otis Taylor was snatched away from the NFL in much the same manner.

But even without Gabriel, Lamar was steadfast, and eventually a TV network contract put millions in the AFL coffers, which in turn gave it a big pot to sign name players out of the NCAA.

Because of that TV contract and Lamar's staying power, it eventually led to a secret meeting with Tex Schramm of the Dallas Cowboys. And it was at that clandestine meeting the two of them put together the rudiment understanding of an agreement. The Hunt-Schramm summit at the Dallas airport was probably the turning point of a very emotional time in sports and for the fans, who were either NFL or AFL loyalists. It still exists deep in the hearts of some of us.

We drafted and got some very good players prior to the merger, though. Players like Johnny Robinson, Buck Buchanan, Bobby Bell and Dave Hill. In the early going, Dave was always getting blamed when Len Dawson got sacked. It got so bad that many were suggesting that it was Hill who invented the so-called "look-out block." It was said that Hill would make the block, then yell, "Lookout, Lenny!"

Another interesting development that has been pretty much understated in the history of the NFL and AFL is the emergence of Al Davis with the Oakland Raiders. He began as an assistant coach with the San Diego Chargers before he went to Oakland as a coach and general manager. From there he eventually gained control and ownership of the franchise. Al has a great mind for making money and has probably made more of it than most in the NFL. There are a lot of Raider Haters in this world, and even though I count myself as one of them, I admire Al Davis a great deal. We have always gotten along pretty well. He has his style, and you can't argue with that. If you look back, the Raiders have been quite successful and run very well.

It was three years before I felt the Chiefs were able to turn the corner in Kansas City. First, many of the players never wanted to leave their homes in Texas to come to what they considered nothing more than a prairie town. In fact, the big joke when they moved up was that they were going to have to live in a place called "Prairie Village." They thought that was the funniest name for a community they could imagine.

The Chiefs lost like six straight games right in the middle of their first season here and didn't do much better record-wise the second season when they finished 7-7. It wasn't until 1966 that attitudes with the players and the community began to mesh.

The Chiefs were in the AFL Championship Game in 1966 in Buffalo. As a gift, Lamar sent all the wives to New York for the game. It seemed to have a big impact on the players, because the Chiefs won that game and went on to play the NFL Champion in the first Super Bowl in Los Angeles. Only they didn't call it the Super Bowl then, it was called the World Championship Game.

After the Chiefs whomped Buffalo 31-7, we all went back to the Holiday Inn where we were staying and gathered around a TV to watch the game between the Green Bay Packers and Dallas Cowboys. There were no fancy hotels back in those days, and it was quite a scene in this old motel in Buffalo, New York.

Everybody except Lamar was drinking up a storm watching the game. Lamar was very stoic and normal, except that somebody had cut his tie in two. But he still had it on.

Back home in Kansas City, the excitement was really starting to boil as people realized that this was the first time in any major sport that their team would be involved in the world championship. It had never occurred, and people streamed to the airport to meet our plane when it came back from Buffalo.

When we approached old Municipal Airport, the pilot came on the intercom and told us we were going to have to circle a couple times to burn off some fuel. Nobody could figure out why. He then told us there were about 10,000 people on the runway at the airport. Everybody was incredulous that a crowd might gather like that.

From that point on, there has always been a love bond between this city and the Chiefs. Of course, there have been many years since when that love has been stretched, but like any good marriage, it's always about a love-hate relationship.

The players from that first Super Bowl became very special members of our Kansas City community, many of whom stayed with the team through the Super Bowl victory after the 1969 season and into early 1970s.

When the Chiefs advanced to that first Super Bowl against the Packers, the game was officially called the World Championship Game, which is how the tickets were printed for the first three games. It wasn't until the fourth game in Tulane Stadium that the tickets bore the Super Bowl title, but even then they were printed as the Fourth World Championship Game Super Bowl. By the time the fifth game was played in Miami's Orange Bowl, however, the World Championship Game had finally been removed and it was simply known as Super Bowl V.

It had been casually referred to as the Super Bowl by the fans in the weeks leading up to the first game. It was Lamar who unofficially gave it the name when he came across his daughter's "super ball."

He made a casual mention of it in the media.

"Why not call our championship game the Super Bowl?" he said, and it found immediate acceptance with the fans, if not the NFL hierarchy.

Tom Hedrick had been my broadcast partner the entire season the Chiefs and Packers played in the first World Championship Game. But as soon as we got to Los Angeles, Tom got an offer from the CBS Radio Network to be a sideline reporter. Even though he had spent the whole season with the Chiefs, he never hesitated and took the CBS job, leaving me without a partner. We brought in Bruce Rice, a very popular sportscaster on KCMO-TV and a good friend. I had worked with Bruce on Missouri football so it was a very easy transition. I did the play-by-play on the Super Bowl and Bruce supplied the color.

I never could figure out, though, why Hedrick would want to bail out in the biggest game of the season for a miserable $50 or whatever he got for working with CBS. Maybe he thought it would lead to a big break with the network or something. In any case, he not only did it for the first Super Bowl, but again for Super Bowl IV.

What a week leading up to that first game. Although it was nothing like it is today, there was a lot of partying going on. A group of us, including Bruce, Pete Carter, Jack Steadman and I

Shortly after winning Super Bowl IV against the Minnesota Vikings, the Chiefs received a ticker-tape parade in downtown Kansas City. Coach Hank Stram holds up the Vince Lombardi Trophy while Otis Taylor, Jack Steadman, Len Dawson and I look on.

went to the Century Plaza Hotel one night, for instance, to catch a performance of Louie Prima and Keely Smith. Joe Bishop's brother was the maitre d' and we had a ball.

Carter owned the Cock 'N Bull Steak House and Lounge on 10th Street in Kansas City. He was very passionate about the Chiefs and the Missouri Tigers and constantly wore black and gold while he was in LA. He was on the bus the Sunday morning we were headed to the Coliseum. He leaned over to me and asked, "Bill, can I come up to the broadcast booth with you?"

"Pete, I don't have credentials for you, and I'm sure you'll need them."

He had a ticket to get into the game but wanted to be an inside part of the whole thing. So when we got there, he marched with me right up to the media gate. Sure enough, the gatekeeper questioned him about his credentials. Both of us tried to con the guy.

"Pete, I know you had it. Did you leave it back at the hotel?" I said.

"Yeah, that's right Bill, it's back at the hotel."

The guy never bit, even though we argued with him a couple minutes later. Finally, I told him I couldn't wait any longer and went up to the radio booth to get ready for pregame. He told me not to worry, he'd figure something out, and I headed up the elevator.

Several hours later I was busy doing the game and I looked down to the Chiefs' bench area and who was sitting on the team bench? Pete Carter, complete with his Chiefs' jacket and black and gold MU driving cap.

After I had left Pete he happened to run into Hank's children, who took him to the locker room. Once they were there they all decided they wanted to watch the game from the bench. But once they got out there the security guard told them they couldn't. That's when Stram himself intervened.

"Look, if you don't let them sit here on the bench, there's not going to be a game here today..."

That was Hank. Always making the big play.

I always kidded Pete about that the rest of his life. He had been begging to go with me and instead he ended up right on top of the action in one of the most historic games ever in sports.

Going into the game, the Packers were heavy favorites. But our whole AFL contingent felt the Chiefs had a pretty darn good chance of winning. They were only behind by four points at the half, 14-10, but in the second half Green Bay blitzed and got to Lenny, and that suddenly turned everything around.

Later when NFL Films produced a program on the game, it really got to a lot of people who had supported the Chiefs. John Fazenda was the longtime narrator for NFL Films and it greatly agitated Hank when he saw it for the first time and heard Fazenda boom out the narrative.

"...the Packers attacked the soft underbelly of the Chiefs..."

That next summer at training camp up at William Jewell College in Liberty, Missouri, Hank showed the Chiefs the film several days before they were to play the NFL Chicago Bears in a preseason game at Municipal Stadium.

The result was predictable. The Chiefs crushed Chicago 66-24. The Chiefs could have scored 100 points that night. When the two teams were walking off the field, Abe Gibron, an assistant with the Bears under George Halas, went over to Stram.

"You shouldn't have done it to the old man," he whispered in his ear.

The truth, though, was the AFL teams at that time were superior to the ones in the old NFL. That was borne out in the head-to-head match-ups of the teams over the next decade. From 1970 through 1979, the old AFL teams won 230 games to the NFL's 184.

"It's not something to really gloat about, but I'm very proud of it," Lamar said. "I keep a running total in my office and I'm always psychologically pulling for the AFC team."

Of course, everybody's expectations for the Chiefs after the first Super Bowl appearance and after the Chiefs had waxed the Bears in preseason were that the Chiefs would return every year to the championship game. The team had a great coach in Stram and players like Dawson, Budde, Headrick, Arbanas, Robinson, Jim Tyrer, Bobby Bell.

Those guys were the Chiefs' stars of the late 1960s and they were a whole lot different from the ones in this century. A lot of the guys had come from Dallas and were pretty tough guys, ones who hit the beer joints pretty hard. Consequently they got a reputation of being partygoers.

And Sherrill was the leader of the pack. He also was a master bridge player, but he was definitely a master drinker. Often before games, he would get the dry heaves. He was great at that, and when he got started he sounded like some kind of animal in distress or something out of *Jurassic Park*. The rookies would pale down by Sherrill's antics.

The Chiefs were playing a game one year in the mid-'60s at Shea Stadium against the New York Jets. It was a frigid day and the Chiefs were on defense. All of a sudden, a couple of us noticed this odd steam rising from the defensive huddle. It looked like they had some kind of fire coming up the middle of the huddle. We found out later that Sherrill had peed in his pants. I asked him about it on the plane ride home, and he said it was the warmest he had been all day.

Of course, all those guys back then played hurt, especially Sherrill. In one game, he got a thumb jammed back into his hand, and when he came running over to the sideline nobody could pull it out because it sickened everyone so much, including Wayne Rudy. Hedrick finally had to do it himself.

Many of the players were on amphetamines—bennies—in the early days of the AFL. They had to be, because they were playing hurt, and if they didn't play, they weren't on the team and had no paycheck or savings. Every player had a handful of bennies most of the time.

It was a different time. Another substance that was later banned was stick 'em, a gooey cream that receivers put on their hands to help them hold onto the football in much the same way George Brett used pine tar on his bat.

I saw guys go into the end zone with the football stuck to their helmets. Gloster Richardson used to spread that stuff all over himself. One time, he patted Hank on the head and Hank's wig came off.

Probably the one game many people will never forget is the Chiefs' marathon Christmas day game against the Miami Dolphins in 1971. It was the one that Kansas City lost in three overtimes, 27-24. Many believe that to be the franchise's greatest ever team. The Chiefs went into the game 10-2-1.

Fran was mad that day, as were many wives all over the city because the NFL was playing on the holiday. It not only postponed Christmas dinner in the afternoon, but all day and long into the night. There are so many memories of that day, but the one that stands out above all the rest is the day that Ed Podolak had. It was one of the greatest single performances I can recall.

But what most people remember, unfortunately, about that double-overtime loss, was Jan Stenerud's missed 31-yard field goal at the end of regulation. Few recall that five years later in an eerily similar circumstance in Miami, Stenerud kicked a 34-yard field goal to give the Chiefs a 20-17 overtime victory over the Dolphins.

"I know what this must mean for Jan, because I know how much it must have hurt him in 1971," said Paul Wiggin, the Chiefs' coach at the time. "I know I wasn't around for that game, but I sure can identify with what happened then and what happened tonight. I've heard about that game so many times. I've read so much about it."

I am not sure the Chiefs of that era ever recovered fully from what happened that day. It was, I believe, also a turning point for Hank Stram. His great players were hitting an age where they were starting on their career downsides. Hank knew it, I think, and then started making some bad trades.

By 1973, the Chiefs had gone from the Christmas Day misery to being 7-5 and very much the mediocre team the record indicated. A year later, losing had set in, Stram's Chiefs falling to 5-9 the next three straight seasons. It hit rock bottom in '77 with a 2-12 record. The Chiefs won only two more games in '78, and it was evident that Hank was going to get fired. Only he didn't realize it.

But Hank had never had a very good grasp of reality much over the course of the previous five years. I don't think also being the general manager helped him, either. He was trying to sign players and coach them at the same time, and in at least one instance it backfired on him terribly.

Once defensive lineman Curly Culp wanted a raise based on what other linemen were making around the league. But Hank wouldn't listen to him, much less give it to him. Curley was incensed. He knew Hank kept his car keys on the top of one his tires, so one day Curley had had just about all he wanted of Hank, went to the parking lot after practice, got Hank's keys and headed to the stadium. Curly threw them down the elevator shaft, but I guess Hank was lucky he didn't get thrown down with them.

There were a series of incidents that Hank misplayed, including keeping some of his veteran players far too long past their prime.

There was a rather interesting meeting a week before Hank got fired. John Sullivan, who was head of the Chiefs' Red Coaters Club, cornered Lamar at the Stadium about how difficult it had become selling season tickets. He told Lamar that something radical had to be done. Lamar paused and simply said the two of them would meet the following week. I thought it rather odd at the time and had a certain feeling about the way Lamar had said that.

By the same time the next week, Lamar had fired Hank.

The 51-year-old Hank was rocked to his soul. He had lost his team and the long association he had had with Lamar. It is hard to imagine that it wasn't the most difficult time of his life the day he got fired from the Chiefs. It was tough, very tough.

"I would be very remorseful if we had never succeeded," he said a couple months later. "But when you were involved in world championships, you've got to feel good about that fact and not dwell on the negative.

"There was no question in my mind that we were on the way back to winning another. You realize the fans are going to forget, but you always hope your people are going to remember and that they're not going to panic. But when they do…"

Hank wasn't away from the sidelines long, becoming the coach of the New Orleans Saints in early 1976. It was Lamar who had recommended The Mentor to Saints owner John Mecom. Hank signed a five-year contract worth more than $1 million.

Ironically, one of the Chiefs' first games later that fall was against Stram and the Saints at Arrowhead. It was a highly charged game for everyone. The Saints led 20-17 with less than a minute to play when Stram called a timeout. The Saints had the ball deep in Kansas City territory and only 14 second to play. Henry wanted to score another touchdown to humiliate Jack Steadman and the new coach, Paul Wiggin.

The Saints scored and Wiggin refused to meet Stram on the field after the game. Stram, meanwhile, ordered rookie Chuck Muncie to give Wiggin an "I Told You So" poster as the Kansas City coach was walking to the locker room. The other New Orleans players had hoisted Stram on their shoulders and were carrying him across the field to a chorus of Kansas City boos.

"I have nothing but good vibrations for Kansas City," Stram tried to explain a couple days later. "It was primarily directed at two people, and neither one of them was Paul or Lamar."

He further explained that the barb was directed at Steadman and Jim Schaaf.

"It's a sad day when you can't do what you feel in your heart, and I did what was in my heart."

Today, Hank and Lamar are friends. Something like the game incident might have destroyed a lot of friendships, and it nearly did that one. But in the end, it worked itself out. Besides, Hank went on to accomplish some things with New Orleans before being fired again in 1978 after a feud with Mecom. But Henry wasn't done yet. He got to feed his ego by doing the NFL Monday Night Games on CBS Radio and became quite popular as a broadcaster.

Hank is a survivor, but some were not.

There have been some painful tragedies within the Chiefs family. Running back Stone Johnson died after an injury in a preseason game shortly after the team moved here from Dallas. Then running back Mack Lee Hill died after an injury. The biggest heartbreak was when Jim Tryer killed his wife and then himself after his several failed business deals. It rocked the community when 17-year-old Brad Tyrer found his parents' bodies in the early morning hours of September 15, 1980.

Few people knew that years earlier in the Chiefs' old training facility on 63rd Street in Swope Park that Tyrer had looked down the barrel of a pistol, aimed at him by a Kansas City teammate.

Tyrer and little-used running back Gene Thomas had gotten in a squabble in the training room. It had something to do with one of their wives being insulted. After they were pulled apart, Thomas a short time later produced a gun, pointed at the Chiefs' big lineman and pulled the trigger. It was never certain whether the gun misfired, it never had been loaded, or whether Thomas just wanted to scare Tyrer.

In any case, the gun was taken from Thomas and the incident never reported to police. Thomas was traded, but returned to the Chiefs later when Tyrer gave his approval of his return.

There have been other untimely deaths of players from the Stram era. Reg Carlton, a tight end, died young. George Daney, another offensive lineman, was found dead in the garage, overcome by carbon monoxide. We have lost Aaron Brown, Jerry Mays and from a later era, All-Pro running back Joe Delaney drowned while trying to save some youngsters.

Later, even Lenny was touched by tragedy when his first wife, Jackie, died in December of 1978 at age 42. It was a tremendous blow to Leonard. But you find out about the calling for a man when he faces such adversity. When Jackie suffered a stroke the year before, he went to beauty school just to be able to fix her hair for her.

"It's such a sad thing when someone so young is taken," said Lamar when he was told. "I had seen her earlier in the fall and she looked so good, and Len seemed so encouraged about her rehabilitation."

Even though Lenny had risen to the heights of the NFL, the trip for both the quarterback and his wife had been a rough one at times.

"It's been a good life, but it's been difficult, too," she said before her death. "It's hard for a young wife to be mature enough to cope with a husband who is in the spotlight when you are not. It's not until you decide that he is your life that you can put everything together. I feel sorry for the young wives."

Earlier the same fall when Jackie died, we also lost our good friend, sportscaster and Chiefs color commentator, Bruce Rice.

Bruce suffered a heart attack while he and the Chiefs were in Pittsburgh, only it wasn't diagnosed until he got back from the road trip. He died the next day on Halloween. The next week the Chiefs were home against the hated Raiders. Oakland won the game, 20-10, and in a surprisingly sensitive gesture, Coach John Madden had the game ball presented to the Chiefs in memory of Bruce. Earlier in the week, the team had renamed the press club at Arrowhead Stadium in honor of Rice.

Of course, Lamar brought other sports to Kansas City in the early going besides professional football, and later the Wizards. He and Norma were big tennis players back home in Dallas, and because of that personal interest they created and pumped money into a new professional circuit called World Championship Tennis, or WCT.

Lamar Hunt is nothing if not an entrepreneurial innovator.

Almost from the beginning, I was intimately involved with the Chiefs and Lamar's revolutionary WCT when it came to Kansas City for two years beginning in 1976.

Besides broadcasting the Chiefs, I was also working for Interstate Securities and Paul Hamilton in the mid-1970s. Lamar went to Paul and asked if he could borrow me for a while to put on the World Doubles Championship at Municipal Auditorium. Lamar had already staged a successful singles tournament in Dallas. The doubles tournament already had a history, having been played in Montreal, Mexico City and Dallas. But low attendance in each of those venues eventually brought it to the Midwest for a final test before Lamar would scrap the idea.

As tournament chairman, I was the front man for the office down at the Westin, and the press came in from all over the world for the tournament the two years that it was held here. It was a first-class event with the championship trophies being created by Waterford Crystal of Ireland.

And, of course, for those two years we had the biggest names in the doubles game...Stan Smith, Arthur Ashe, Vijay Amritraj, Tony Roche, Vitas Gerulaitis, Tom Okker, Wojtek Fibak, Bob Lutz, Ilie Nastase, Ken Rosewall.

They were all class athletes. Very friendly and enjoyable to be around. I remember we had a media tournament a few days before the actual doubles competition got started, and it was lots of fun. Some of the pros played with us hackers, but they treated us well and, of course, didn't give it their best shot. Even Nastase, Mr. Nasty, was very much a gentleman. And even though there was a large international press corps including NBC's Bud Collins, it was a local media team that won the media tournament, Ken Rudnick and Gene Fox of *The Kansas City Star*.

There was a small controversy concerning the foreign journalists covering the five-day event. The WCT picked up the tab to have them come to Kansas City, costing about $18,000. Some claimed the reporters had been bought off, but Lamar did a great job of justifying the expense.

"We'd rather not spend the money obviously, but we're trying to establish something that's known worldwide," he said. "Nothing starts at a peak. In many ways, it's like some of the things that are done in football. There is a press party at the Super Bowl that costs over $200,000."

In the end, I am not convinced that the pros fully cooperated with Lamar in his efforts to make the WCT in general a viable professional series. Lamar was one of the guys who stuck his neck out to increase the players' purses. But the players weren't all that responsive in supporting and participating in both the singles series or doubles events leading up to the championship events. Eventually Lamar backed away.

The qualifying tournaments were held all over the world, with the doubles championship being staged the first two years in Montreal. But total attendance was just over 20,000 and they were moved first to Mexico then to Texas, where attendance was just as lukewarm. WCT officials thought that the Midwest might embrace the concept because of the strong tennis community here that included Marvin Richmond, president of the United States Tennis Association.

"Middle America!" exclaimed Ron Walker, a WCT associate director. "They love it."

Lamar had brought in Walker to assist in our Kansas City operation. Walker had been a secretary in the Richard Nixon White House. Walker had a long list of responsibilities with the administration, not the least of which was arranging Nixon's trip to China. Walker was very accomplished, having overcome extreme political and cultural differences in getting Nixon behind the Great Wall. The Midwest, seemingly, would be an overhead slam.

I really enjoyed working with Walker, and, boy, could he slam down the martinis. I thought I was good, but Walker put me to shame. He was a real martini pro. Walker must have had a cast iron stomach because the drinking didn't seem to affect him at all. I guess that's what you became working with somebody like Nixon. I remember one night he had six to my one.

One day the phone rang in the office, and I'll never forget it.

"Yeah, this is (Chuck) Colson, let me speak to Ron Walker."

I gave the phone to Ron, and later he would tell me that Colson had been calling from a federal penitentiary, where he was serving time for his part in the Watergate cover-up. Ron talked about the whole thing openly to me. He even told me he had tried to convince Nixon to destroy all the Watergate tapes, but Nixon was afraid to because he believed there were other copies and eventually he would get nailed for destroying evidence.

Walker fascinated me and I would have to say we enjoyed working together a great deal. But not even the guy who was able to penetrate the Great Wall of China could make the World Doubles Championship a success in Kansas City. The World Doubles was a great idea and concept, but we just couldn't draw enough people to make it work here or get the business community to put up the necessary $100,000 for a local package. That's not much of an investment today, but remember this was the middle 70s, and the economy was a little flat. Both Lamar and I together made numerous calls to the business community, but, ultimately, we could not get enough people involved.

Only 3,971 die-hard fans showed up for the championship finals in 1978 when Wojtek Fibak and Tom Okker beat Stan Smith and Bob Lutz.

"Now anytime I think about Kansas City, I'll have pleasant thoughts," Fibak said afterwards.

The event only had a two-year run in Kansas City, but I am proud of those two years.

Of course, I enjoyed anything that would promote the town and help fill hotel rooms. I had just been appointed to the Convention and Visitor's Bureau. And now, nearly 40 years later, I am still on the board.

The second year it was held, Lamar and Norma happened to be in Europe at the time. And since the tournament was on one of the national networks, they were able to watch it overseas. So one day I got a call at Municipal Auditorium from Lamar in Innsbruck, Austria. He has always demanded perfection in everything and he had seen something he didn't like.

"Bill, I'm looking at the setup with the little flags on each end of the tennis court," he began, "but the one on the right side is off line…it's off center. Would you mind moving that over just a little bit?"

"Uh, no problem Lamar, I can get that done," I told him.

"Okay, talk to you later."

So I moved it and all was seemingly right with the world. But the phone rang 30 minutes later.

"Bill, that's still off center!"

What had happened was that there were some guys down in the corner and every time I would move it, they would move it back. They either had problems seeing with the flags there, or they had gotten wind of what was happening and were simply being ornery.

Weeks later I got a letter from Lamar thanking me for all my work at the tournament.

"Dear Bill,

"From the time I received the frantic call in Innsbruck from 'Vill Grisley' to the moment Norma and I watched television…I knew we were in great hands. A friend asked me what it's like to work with Grigsby, and I reassured him it's a lot like landing a 747 jet airplane—you know you are never more than 30 seconds away from a disaster!

"Seriously, Bill—many thanks for stepping into the breach in what undoubtedly had to be nervous territory for you (and wasn't N.R. Walker a reassuring factor—after all, you knew that he had guided R.M. Nixon through to safety. "World Doubles, Kansas City and success will become synonymous—and all with WCT are grateful for your participation and help.

"Sincerely,

Lamar"

And who knows, maybe Lamar was the ringleader of the flag incident.

Certainly he was for everything else he touched.

CHAPTER 10

The Chiefs' Losing Years

In the years since Hank Stram's departure, no one has matched the glory he brought to Kansas City.

Not Marv Levy. Not Marty Schottenheimer. Not Dick Vermeil.

That is not to say the coaches who have come and gone were not as good or even better coaches. Certainly, each has offered his own brand of excitement.

There have been exciting games, perhaps, even better teams than those of the Stram era. Fan expectation has been as high, maybe, even higher at certain times. And who is to say that the disappointments haven't been as deep as in some losses, and seasons, than those when Henry was storming the sideline with his rolled-up game plan. No season ever seems to have created as much expectation but ended with more disappointment than the 2003-04 season, one when the Chiefs won their first nine games and finished 13-3, only to lose to the Indianapolis Colts in the first-round playoff game.

But no matter how you rationalize it, no one...not Levy, Schottenheimer or Vermeil...has taken the Chiefs to the top of the National Football League. The only coach to have done that for Kansas City is Hank Stram.

That is not to censure the current era. It is a great one, just as dedicated as the first-generation coaching and administrative brain trust. But we have experienced a great many faces and game plans between where this franchise is now and where it began.

If the last decade and a half have been the greatest for the Chiefs in terms of winning percentage, the 15 years between the Stram era and today could only be described as mediocre. And that's being generous. The mid-section of Chiefs history is burdened by such average and forgettable players as Arnold Morgado, Zenon Andrusyshyn, Jimbo Elrod, Cliff Frazier, Chuck Zapiec, Dave Rozumek, Horace Belton, Steve Stropolo. Seemingly the list is endless, as were the losses. Some of the names represent a stain on Chiefs history.

The parade of mediocrity got so bad that in the spring of 1979, the Chiefs opened Arrowhead for a public tryout. The Chiefs' roster was so thin, the team actually signed four free agents from that tryout: wide receivers Stanley Sam and Rory Henning and linemen James Emerson and Kurtis Jonker.

All too often the headlines after Chiefs games told the story of the era.

- Steelers Add To Chiefs' Misery, 30-3, November 12, 1979.
- Chiefs Now 0-4 and No Relief in Sight, October 10, 1977.
- 'No Timeout' Call Costs Chiefs, November 7, 1978.
- Chiefs Resort to Ploy, October 17, 1975.
- Penalties Put Chiefs in Hole, October 17, 1978.
- What Will Happen Next to Chiefs? November 20, 1978.

It got so bad one year that a frustrated Hunt did a very uncharacteristic Lamar thing; he telephone the bench during a game.

"He wanted to know how things were going and why we didn't have the right number of players on the field," said Steve

Ortmayer, special teams coach, after the Chiefs had lost 23-7 to the Denver Broncos in 1977.

Others in the locker room were not so friendly.

"I have nothing to say," barked Morgado, the back-up full-back.

"I would appreciate it if you would not ask me for comment," pleaded guard Tom Condon.

Lamar and Jack Steadman opted for a different coaching formula than had succeeded with Hank Stram. Instead of going back into the college ranks they sought out a rah-rah guy from the NFL assistant ranks. But as it turned out, maybe Paul Wiggin was a bit too raw-raw for the rough-and-tumble NFL. Wiggin, an assistant at San Francisco, was named as the Chiefs' new head coach on January 23, 1975, a month after Stram was fired.

Paul's first season was 1975, and he arrived with a good record on the Pacific Coast. From the start he was heralded as the guy who was going to bring the team back together and be the big winner it once was. Of course, it never happened. Paul just never got out of the starting blocks. It was never exactly clear why he didn't do better here, except it probably had to do with the quarterback position.

Paul Wiggin had a great defensive mind, but remember he had been left with a legacy of aging veterans. He was also burdened by the fact that not a single draft choice from 1975 was able to make the team, an indictment of General Manager Jim Schaaf as much as anybody, perhaps.

But as it turned out, Wiggin, who as a player himself had been an All-Pro twice, just wasn't head coach material. It was an awkward position for Paul, as typified by the fact that he was left to try to talk linebacker Willie Lanier and defensive back Kerry Reardon out of retirement. I think Paul always regretted that decision and it illustrated just how bad the problem was. Many of the veterans, including Kerry, had some value left, but their skills had eroded and they did not offer what their experience might have indicated otherwise.

"Willie was the first great black middle linebacker," Wiggin said once during his tenure.

"He's been in several Pro Bowls. He's been a world champion. He has done it all, and there wasn't much left for Willie," Wiggin continued, hinting Lanier lacked motivation.

Some of the other aging veterans were linebacker Jim Lynch, cornerback Emmitt Thomas and Buck Buchanan. The Chiefs had also gotten John Matuzak, but he got into so much trouble while he was in Kansas City, Wiggin eventually had to get him out of town.

The aging veterans also cost Wiggin his best friend. He got into an argument one day after practice with defensive coordinator Vince Costello about whether the veterans should be playing instead of some of the rookies. Costello and Wiggin were extremely close, having played side by side with the Browns from 1957 through 1967. Costello was Wiggin's first assistant hired, and the first to leave. Embittered by the fight, Vince abruptly walked out and opened Costello's Greenhouse Restaurant that was at the corner of Ward Parkway and 87th Street for many years.

"I could have done with the Chiefs what I did with the restaurant if I had been given the chance," Costello said.

We all should have seen the situation for what it was at the time: a team headed downhill instead of up. But whether you are a broadcaster, fan, coach or the general manager, I think there is the tendency to see things in a positive frame of mind rather than looking at it realistically.

Len Dawson was in the final years of his career, although Mike Livingston was doing most of the quarterbacking at this stage. Not doing a very good job, I might add.

I actually was doing the public address for the stadium while Wiggin was the coach. I was involved with the hockey Scouts and took a two-year absence from the Chiefs' broadcasts. I did, however, produce the radio broadcasts. Al Wisk was the play-by-play man and Bruce Rice the color announcer in my absence. Bruce became exceedingly close to Paul, maybe too close. Wiggin was a very nice person, and it pained us all to see him go in such an abrupt way.

Actually, the team's biggest weapon during those days was probably kicker Jan Stenerud, but, after all, how many field goals could he have kicked to save games? The Chiefs blistered the Cleveland Browns 39-14 in the final game of 1976 on December 12, but there were nearly 16,000 no-shows in the stands. The attendance for that game was only 34,340, the smallest regular-season crowd since the Chiefs had moved into Arrowhead Stadium. The Chiefs' next-door neighbors, the Royals, were easily attracting more fans to their baseball games.

After the '76 season, one of the beloved greats of the Stram era did hang it up after a spectacular 14-year career, guard Ed Budde. "Bluto" as some had nicknamed him, was a former All-Pro who had represented everything that was right about the franchise in its early history and pro football. Later his son, Brad, would also be a first-round draft choice out of Southern Cal and play a major role with the Chiefs.

"For 14 years it's been good," he said the day after practice when he announced his plans. "I've been good for the Kansas City Chiefs, and they've been good for me."

When the next season rolled around, "Bluto" was gone, and the coach would be soon.

The crewcut Wiggin lasted seven games into the 1977 season, being fired after the team lost 44-7 to the Browns, Paul's old team that he had helped win a world championship in 1964. Wiggin was a great defensive mind, but aging veterans hamstrung him. The bottom line on Paul Wiggin is he just was never able to get out of the starting blocks. He was fired, compiling a miserable 11-24 record.

Lamar and Steadman made Tom Bettis the interim coach to finish out the season. Tom was a great friend who Wiggin had kept from Stram's old coaching staff. But Tom was your quintessential career assistant in much the same way Frank Ganz and Gunther Cunningham were. He was a great assistant coach but should have never considered aspiring to become a head coach.

Interestingly, the Chiefs beat the Green Bay Packers 20-10 in Bettis's first game as coach, but the team awarded Wiggin the game ball.

"I'm still hurting," he said when Bettis took him the ball. "And I'm still under the porch like a wounded dog."

Tom was promised a fair evaluation at the end of the season and was assured he would get every consideration to become the permanent coach should he do well. I don't believe that was ever going to be the case, that Tom's days with the franchise were numbered as soon as Wiggin got the axe. Bettis did an admirable job the rest of the way, but I don't think even he believed he would be around long after the season ended since he finished out 1-6.

"Until you start winning games, you don't overcome the negatives," Lamar said after the season. "I don't remember any season with so many negatives. When we're losing, everything turns sour. The hotdogs are colder, the parking lots are less managed, and it just seems everything is wrong."

No, there weren't any indications that Tom Bettis would be asked back.

He wasn't.

The rumor mill went wild with speculation about who would become the Chiefs' next coach. Monte Clark, the former coach at San Francisco, seemed to be the leading candidate, although Ara Parseghian and Barry Switzer were also mentioned.

But the Chiefs and Lamar went into the Canadian Football League to find their next coach, who eventually would make it into the NFL Hall of Fame, not because of his tenure with the Chiefs, but the Buffalo Bills. He had been recommended to Jack Steadman by George Allen, coach of the Washington Redskins.

Marv Levy, who had just won the Grey Cup Championship in the CFL, was introduced to the Kansas City media just before Christmas 1977, as the team's fourth head coach. There was much ballyhoo and expectation when Marv and his wife, Dorothy, were brought to Kansas City.

Marv, who resembled comedian Pat Paulsen, was an extremely likable and unique coach because of his intellect. He was a student of history and would often quote and equate battle with the struggles of teams in the NFL. His college degree was in English and he also had taught English at Coe College in Iowa, so his credentials were considerably different than the NFL coaching fraternity. He also had been a Phi Beta Kappa.

"I went to college at Coe and later to Harvard for graduate school with the idea to be a lawyer," he said. "I went for about six weeks in Cambridge but then withdrew. I wanted to coach, and now I don't have a regret in the world."

His first coaching job was at St. Louis Country Day School, and his team finished 13-1 in his first season.

Before training camp began, the Chiefs lost another star from the glory years. Running back Ed Podolak announced his retirement during the summer after nine years with the club.

The annual 101 Banquet is always a fun time. One year, I got together with Ed Podolak and Mike Ditka.

"Losing has had a big emotional impact on me the last couple of years," he said. "I had not been happy, and at this point of my career, I didn't think I could handle more losing."

The 51-year-old Levy did a masterful job of turning the Chiefs' fortunes around on and off the field. His first year the Chiefs went 7-9, which was a big improvement, while the team was putting people back in the stadium once again. The next year, the record improved to 8-8, and there was a strong belief that things were headed upward. Levy had taken a basic, simplistic approach by using the wing-T offense.

Then came the next season, and the year the players went on strike. Remember the movie, *The Replacements,* starring Keanu Reaves? Well, we lived a real-life version of the ineptitude of bringing in scab players. The strike was a disaster, and the season became a disaster.

I remember we went to Los Angeles with the replacement players to play the Raiders' subs. The night before the game, there was a minor earthquake and we all had to be evacuated from the hotel at one o'clock in the morning, and then the next day the temperature got up in the upper 90s during the game. The whole experience was awful.

Dawson and I had just finished a nightcap and gone to our rooms when the earthquake hit. I remember lying down in bed, and the whole room shaking. I thought to myself, "Wow, I wonder what was in that last drink!"

Actually, I never left my room when they ordered everybody out; I was on one of the lower floors of the 20-story hotel. I figured that if it came down, it wouldn't make any difference whether I was standing in the parking lot or lying in my bed. So, I just simply rolled over and went to sleep.

Marv was the coach for the debacle, and situations like that would drive the man wild. He was sort of a Jeckel-Hyde. Away from the stadium and the game, Marv was eloquent and cerebral, quoting from great authors or historical events. He came across as very scholarly. But on the sidelines, you wouldn't believe what might come out of his mouth when he didn't like a play or the call of an official. He definitely had an X-rated football vocabulary. There was no way you could put a microphone on him during a game.

"I can't say any more without being in violation of the league rules and getting myself a heavy fine," he told the press after a 28-6 loss to the Raiders.

I remember after one especially excruciating loss, Joe McGuff and I walked by his office and he was actually screaming and beating his head on the wall. We were really worried about him, and we thought we would give him another five minutes, and if he was still doing it, we might go to his aid.

Well, several minutes went by, the screaming stopped and all of a sudden he pops out of his office and says, "Hi, guys!" and walks past us into the pressroom for the postgame news conference. Joe and I just looked at each other and shook our heads.

Toward the end of his Kansas City term, more often than not he would greet the media following losses with a glassy stare in his eyes, as though he had just been struck by lightening. He was trying extremely hard to mask his frustration.

"There's this great big snake crawling around out there someplace," he once said after a loss, "and it bites us every time we go out.

"We play reasonably well but find ways to lose. It reminds me of the old joke when the reporter asks Mary Lincoln, 'Other than what happened, Mrs. Lincoln, how did you enjoy the play?'"

It was during the Levy era when I was doing the postgame interviews in the locker room. It could be very difficult to find guys to even talk to after some of those heartbreaking losses. Sometimes the only guys I could pester into talking were the ones who felt they might have a broadcasting career after they got out of football. I remember nose tackle Bill Maas was always one of my favorites, and today as a broadcaster he is doing quite nicely with his new career with the Fox Sports Network.

One time, when we lost a game on the last play, I said later during the locker room show that, "I'm too old to cry and too sick to puke." CBS picked that up and used it."

Eventually, when Marv was fired it was something of a surprise and maybe not a very good decision considering that he eventually went to several Super Bowls as the Bills coach. But again, the decision to dump Marv was not so much about his potential or even coaching ability at the time, but the lack of fans in the stands. There was something like 11,000 left in 80,000-seat Arrowhead at the end of Marv's final game with the Chiefs. There is no way somebody like Jack Steadman and Lamar Hunt were going to accept or tolerate that. Lamar is now drawing that for Wizards soccer. That's great for soccer, but totally unacceptable for the NFL and unheard of by today's standards. The plain truth of the matter is that if the Chiefs do well, the city does well. After a win on Sunday, the bar business is good, the restaurant business is good, the city's economy is good.

The year Marv was fired, the Chiefs, with the interruption for the strike, were 3-6 and finished 11th in the NFL. Overall, Marv was 31-42 with Kansas City.

A cocky Dallas Cowboy assistant was hired to replace Levy. John Mackovic and his wife, Arlene, were the next NFL darlings to get the "can't miss" label when they were introduced. Mackovic's star had risen as the Cowboys' prominence had spread as America's Team in the early eighties. He was the latest touted young wunderkind and was in moderate demand.

John arrived in 1983 and carried a confidence not seen since Hank strutted the Kansas City sidelines. He was a friend and quite personable. I was supportive.

And speaking of good friends, another one of the front office personnel during the Wiggin-to-Mackovic period was the team's public relations director, Bob Sprenger, and his assistant, Doug Kelley. The two were considered two of the best and most respected in NFL PR circles. Without a doubt, they were very much liked by not only the local media but the national media as well.

Sprenger had come to Kansas City from the West Coast, where he had been the media guy for the Pac-8. He had become especially close with Wiggin, and felt a deep disappointment when Paul had been fired. But he quickly adjusted to both Levy and now

Mackovic. I remember one off season when Mackovic, Sprenger and I all happened to be in Los Angeles together. We spent a great day together at the Riviera Country Club playing golf. It was a wonderful, memorable day, especially since we coaxed Dan Reaves, coach of the Broncos at the time, to be our fourth.

During Sprenger's tenure with the club, there was a notably close relationship between the broadcasters and newspaper beat reporters. Kelly went on to bigger and better things, and Sprenger hired another top assistant in Gary Heise, who later would take over for Sprenger when Bob took a similar job with the NCAA.

During this time, it was not uncommon for the entire media corps to travel with the team on the charter jets when the Chiefs played on the road. And once in other NFL cities, the media and members of the Chiefs' front office would often dine together the night before the game, the team picking up the dinner tab that routinely would run several thousand dollars.

Afterwards, the media—Sprenger and Kelley, who became known as "Radar"—would often party together, sometimes late into the night. Bob definitely was a press guy's PR dream. Bob was, and still is, a great person to be around because of his jovial and positive nature. Not so surprisingly, he runs his own marketing and public relations firm today in Kansas City.

The press corps that followed the Chiefs in the early and mid years was an extremely close-knit group. Joe McGuff, Tom Marshall, Bill Richardson, Gerald Jordan, Gene Fox, Dick Mackey, Jon Rand, Gib Twyman, and Mike McKenzie were some of the early sportswriters from *The Star* who covered both the good and bad of those days. Bob Hentzen, Steve Cameron, Rick Dean, Dick Fensler and Mark Nusbaum were the regulars from the *Topeka Capital-Journal* while Charlie Smith reported for the Wichita newspaper. Bill Althaus, Dick Puhr and Don Pfannenstiel for the *Independence Examiner*, Rick Gosselin was the UPI correspondent and Doug Tucker was from Associated Press. Frank Boal and Gordon Docking of WDAF-TV, Jack Harry and Bruce Rice of KCMO-TV and Don Fortune and John Sanders were regulars from KMBC-TV.

It was a colorful and diverse group, but one that got along well, considering that they were all competitors.

Probably the newspaper reporter most closely associated with the team through its first years in Kansas City up until Carl Peterson came to town was *The Star*'s Bill Richardson, a soft-spoken and gentle man with a quick wit. Richardson covered every Chiefs game, home and away, for 20 straight seasons.

Once in the early days, while Sprenger was the public relations director, he, Richardson and I were in a San Diego bar waiting for the rest of the media to come down from their hotel rooms. Sprenger had to leave, but asked if we would entertain the rest of the reporters when they arrived. We were staying at the Ocean Side Hotel, a great place.

Bob left and told us if he didn't make it back just to sign the tab and assign it to his room. Well, Sprenger went off about his business and I told Bill to order when the waitress came. He wanted a whiskey and coke.

"Hold it, right there!" I stopped him. "No self-respecting sportswriter from *The Star* would ever order whiskey and coke. Look, if you're going to follow this team and call yourself a newspaper reporter, you can't order coke in your whiskey. Have a martini."

Richardson wouldn't order a martini, but he did from that point on forever drink VO and water. And from that point on, his nickname in our circle became Whiskey Bill.

Our bar tab that afternoon alone, by the way, was something like $600. Then we went to dinner.

The routine would eventually end when Carl Peterson came to town from Philadelphia and brought his own public relations honcho, Bob Moore, who had his own style of running things. The times between Wiggin and Marty Ball were some of the worst for the team, but the best for the media.

But it was fun while it lasted, maybe too much fun. Once on a trip to Washington, D.C., one particularly enthusiastic member of the media got especially rambunctious after dinner. After dining at an exclusive and expensive downtown restaurant, all of us decided to hit the Georgetown scene before retiring for the evening. We told our cabbie to run us by the White House on our way. It was a mistake.

And since the Chiefs were footing the bill for the press dinner, I also started another ritual that was popular with our circle of all-male reporters. After dinner everybody would put a buck in a pot and guess the total bill for the evening. The guys who guessed high and low had to put in an extra dollar. Then the person who was closest to the actual bill received the kitty. The only trouble was, nobody wanted to actually win, because they had to buy the first round of drinks afterward, and that tab always exceeded the amount of the pot.

Once in Houston, instead of guessing the tab amount, we guessed the weight of the waitress who served us in the Mexican restaurant. Somehow we didn't get tossed then or ever, even though some of the younger members of the press got pretty rowdy in some of the nation's finest eating establishments across the country.

Whether it was at the restaurant, hotel or the next day at the game, the press corps would always gather with Sprenger, and we would get a team picture. I've got dozens of those now and they are a treasure. Once we included Dorothy Levy when we were staying at the Berkeley Marina prior to a game with Oakland. I have a shot with fullback MacArthur Lane in Houston and all of us with the Denver Cheerleaders at Mile High City. The Hunts posed with us in San Diego, and in Houston I doubled-back my arm so it looks like I'm a one-armed reporter there.

When we returned from road trips, we had another little game we would play in the media. We'd each throw five dollars in the pot and the reporter whose bag came up first would win. What nobody knew was that I often would give the luggage guys downstairs $20 to send mine up first.

It was those kinds of antics that were the highlights for the media when the Chiefs were going badly. Another highlight was our TWA pilot on the charter flights, Harry Hunzeker who had been nicknamed "Crash" by Bruce Rice. Harry was an excellent pilot who felt very much a part of the Chiefs' family back then. He was also extremely personable and always had little surprises for us whenever we flew somewhere. Once on a trip to the West Coast he dropped down to get a birds'-eye view of the Grand Canyon. Just before we would land in Seattle, he'd take us by to see the climbers on Mt. Rainier.

For the fans during this time, it wasn't the Chiefs who were the exciting part of the game; it was a guy by the name of George Henderson, otherwise known as "Krazy George." The 35-year-old school teacher from Denver was the centerpiece of the Chiefs' marketing campaign and every week the club would fly him in to bang his drum and yell like Howard Dean after the Iowa caucuses.

"As far as I'm concerned, he's the best I've ever seen as far as getting people enthused," Lamar said in 1979. "Both Jack Steadman and Jim Schaaf were very skeptical."

Everybody was pretty much in an upbeat mood with Mackovic's arrival. And although he was considered a bit standoffish, aloof and arrogant, his wife, Arlene, was considered a classy lady who everybody admired and believed kept John under control. She and John were good friends with Al Saunders and his wife. Al, of course, is the offensive coordinator on Vermeil's staff. John and Al had gone to school together.

John, who would not be considered a strong people person, also considered himself something of a food and wine connoisseur, which he liked to indulge when we were on the road.

Mackovic put together some good solid seasons as the Chiefs' coach with Frank Gansz as his special teams coach. Those years were marked by spectacular special teams play when Albert Lewis blocked several punts and ran them back for touchdowns.

What was odd is that Mackovic's predecessors had all been fired after dismal final seasons when crowd attendance had fallen drastically. Mackovic actually got the Chiefs into the playoffs with a 10-6 record, finishing second to 11-5 Denver in the AFC West in 1986. Mackovic put the Chiefs in the playoffs for the first time in 16 years, even though they lost in their first-round game. But shortly after the loss to the New York Jets, John got the ax after what was commonly believed to be a player mutiny against him in favor of Gansz.

Who knows exactly what was Lamar's thinking, but the fact remains that a number of players gathered the day after the play-off loss to the Jets at kicker Nick Lowery's house. Lowery was generally considered the ringleader, and shortly thereafter the players came out publicly and announced their support for their special teams coach, Frank Ganz.

Shortly afterwards, after the palace uprising, Mackovic was indeed out with a 30-34 overall record, and Gansz was in as the Chiefs' head coach.

Gansz was all about enthusiasm and college rah-rah. I think he could have talked a dog off a meat wagon. As a result there was a lot of anticipation about Gansz as a head coach. I know I was excited and curious what he might do. As the season got closer the expectation grew.

"Wake up Bill, it's 20 to 7," Fran said to me one morning in mid-August.

"Who's winning?" I quipped back.

This also was a season when the players went back on strike, which didn't fare well for fan support or Gansz' future. After making the playoffs the year before, the Chiefs finished 4-11 in the strike-interrupted season under Ganz.

I think Lamar and Steadman were skeptical by this time of Ganz but willing to go the extra step the following season. Ganz was on shaky footing at the start of the 1988 season, and if he stumbled out of the gate everybody figured major changes were in store.

The Chiefs lost their first two games, but won the third. Then came the losses; a string of them. Ganz was history after a second straight 11-loss season.

And, so too, was general manager Jim Schaaf and president Jack Steadman. Schaaf was shown the front door while Steadman was kicked upstairs as chairman of the board. It was the biggest shakeup in the club's history.

Lamar brought in a new general manager and president who would greatly impact the future of the franchise and return a large measure of glory to this proud team over the next 15 years.

Carl D. Peterson came to town in 1988, and a new era was about to unfold.

CHAPTER 11

The Peterson Era

When Carl Peterson answered the call from Lamar Hunt in 1988 it marked the beginning of a new and exciting era. Peterson wasted little time in hiring a successful coach from Cleveland—Marty Shottenheimer. It would be the catalyst we'd been waiting for, new enthusiasm, a winning approach, no slogans, just results.

At least we all envisioned that. But wait a minute, we opened that first year losing to Denver, San Diego and Cincinnati and winning only over the Raiders. The blush of victory and a full house at Arrowhead turned pale until the stretch run when the Chiefs won four of the last five games. But even then the 8-7-1 finish was good enough for a second-place finish in the West.

In 1990 the team of Carl and Marty finished second in the West, but this time it was 11-5 and a playoff berth. The thrill was back despite a first-round loss to Miami when Nick Lowery missed a winner after kicking three from the field earlier. It was a bitter 17-16 loss after leading 16 to 3. But the playoff heartbreak the

Carl Peterson and I on an Air Force trip.

Chiefs suffered put them back in the fight, and Arrowhead was full again. Peterson football had arrived as the architect of a new and exciting football powerhouse.

When I heard Carl speak at the first press conference, I sensed he would be successful. He was stepping into the spot vacated by Jack Steadman, who moved up to chairman. He was becoming the president, general manager and CEO and is still around leading one of the most successful programs in the NFL.

The 1992 season represented something of a letdown for Chiefs' fans. The Chiefs again finished second in the AFC West with a 10-6 record but were eliminated in the opening round of the playoffs this time.

During the off season, Peterson pulled off one of the most remarkable coups in team history, acquiring both Joe Montana and Marcus Allen from the San Francisco 49ers and Oakland Raiders. Super Bowl talk was rampant.

The two future Hall of Fame athletes were past their prime, but few doubted that they had enough left in their tanks to elevate the ascending Chiefs into the NFL stratosphere. When the 1993 season kicked off, Kansas City seemed to have it all: Peterson in the front office, Schottenheimer on the sidelines, Montana at quarterback, Allen in the backfield, Derrick Thomas and Neil Smith on defense and, finally, a stadium full of loud, screaming fans.

It was a season to remember. The Chiefs, with an 11-5 record, won the division for the first time in 22 years. It had been an awful drought for the city and especially the dedicated owner of the team. In his fifth year with the franchise, it appeared that Carl Peterson's pledge of returning the Chiefs to the Super Bowl was on track. It had been a solid season for both Montana, who passed for 2,144 yards and 13 touchdowns, and Allen, who rushed for 764 yards and 12 TDs.

Kansas City beat Pittsburgh 27-24 in the first playoff game then dispatched Houston 28-20 before heading to Buffalo for the AFC Championship game against the Bills. The Super Bowl dream was bashed pretty good by the Bills, 30-13.

Both Montana and Allen returned in 1994, but the Chiefs were dethroned as AFC West champions after a 9-7 record. Joe actually had a better season than the year before, passing for 3,283 yards and 16 touchdowns, but he played his final professional game on New Year's Eve against the Dolphins in Miami, where the Chiefs lost their first playoff game 27-17.

Montana had retired, but Peterson strengthened the Chiefs, and they came roaring back with Steve Bono at quarterback in '95. It was one of the most promising seasons in Chiefs history, much like the 2004 campaign. Just like in 04, the Chiefs dominated with a 13-3 record. But if it had been one of the most successful seasons in franchise history, it also ended with one of the most disappointing games ever. The Chiefs stumbled in the opening round to the Indianapolis Colts 10-7.

It was one of the lowest moments ever for the fans, the owner and the president. But as is my trademark, I tried to paint a happy face on the whole debacle. I'm always the guy who reminds fans at the end of the game not to go home and kick the dog and be nice to your wife, cause we're going to come back the following week or season and win. I simply refuse to let a game that I can't control whatsoever mess up my life.

And I am not one to do much second guessing. I often hear network commentators talk about a corner or safety missing an assignment. But I'll let you in on a little secret, a broadcaster can't tell that generally from the booth, especially with today's complicated defensive schemes.

Two years later the Chiefs again were 13-3 and AFC West Champions. But another first-round playoff loss, this time to the Denver Broncos 14-10, caused many to wonder out loud whether Carl Peterson would ever bring the Lombardi Trophy back to Kansas City.

The next few seasons were marked by loss. The community and Peterson, especially, were stunned by the death of All-Pro linebacker Derrick Thomas following a car accident during an ice storm. Carl and Derrick were unusually close. Even though it's not apparent to outsiders, Peterson has a close relationship with a lot of his players. Derrick was something of a project for Carl. Derrick's father had been killed in Vietnam, and Carl sort of became a father figure to him. He was devastated by Derrick's death, and I'm not sure Carl will ever again let a player get as close to him as Thomas did.

Meanwhile, in the mid-1990s, rumors began to swirl about the Chiefs' coach, Marty Schottenheimer, and his motivation and relationship with his players. Schottenheimer eventually resigned in 1998.

Defensive coordinator Gunther Cunningham took over in 1999, but there were considerable doubts about his ability to perform as head coach, especially after a 9-7 season. Part of Gunther's problem was that he worked too hard at coaching. He might spend 20 hours a day at Arrowhead working on game plans, and then on Sunday the Chiefs would lose. What does that tell you if you spend that much time in your office and lose anyway? There was little confidence after the team went 7-9 in 2000, and Gunther was out.

During the off season, Peterson finally got what he had worked his whole life for and what had always been his dream. He got Dick Vermeil on January 12, 2001.

He coaxed his friend and mentor out of a second retirement and a 14-year sabbatical. After a long hiatus from coaching, Vermeil had followed up his Super Bowl appearance in Philadelphia in 1981 by returning to the sidelines in St. Louis in 1996. Three years later, he and the Rams won Super Bowl XXXIV, and then he seemingly retired for good.

Vermeil already has proved to be the best coach the Chiefs have had since Hank. He handles people as well as anyone I have ever seen in the coaching ranks. He can get mad when he thinks somebody is dogging it, but he handles the situation extremely well. I think maybe he learned some of that while he was out of football and in the broadcast booth. I believe being a broadcaster all those years gave him a sense of maturity and allowed him to gain a perspective of the game he otherwise wouldn't have gotten.

Their first season together in Kansas City went as many predicted, with an unspectacular 6-10 record. The following year was 8-8, and you could see the pieces coming together. Peterson and Vermeil had gotten the quarterback they felt was Super Bowl caliber in Trent Green. They had the league's leading rusher in Priest Holmes. Peterson made deals to shore up a suspect defense. Everything seemed to be on track.

Going into the 2003 season, the Chiefs were *Sports Illustrated*'s AFC pick for the Super Bowl. Kick returner Dante Hall got off to a spectacular start running back either four punts or kickoff returns for touchdowns. Trent Green was superb, and Holmes was on a touchdown record run.

The Chiefs won their first nine games, and there was talk of them running the board in a cover story in *SI*. No one honestly blamed the cover jinx of *SI* for the Chiefs' ensuing loss to the Bengals in Cincinnati, because what Peterson, Vermeil and the rest of Kansas City feared most would become blatantly obvious in the coming weeks when the Chiefs were blown out against the Denver

Broncos and Minnesota Vikings when the Kansas City defense played embarrassingly badly.

Throughout most of the 2003 season, the sports talk shows were filled with criticism of defensive coordinator Greg Robinson. It became especially hardened the second half of the season when the Chiefs' defense played with little confidence or effectiveness. Vermeil defended Robinson. But what I was especially impressed with was not what was being said in Robinson's defense, but what wasn't being said.

Not once did Carl Peterson ever publicly criticize the Chiefs' defense, Robinson, or Vermeil's staunch support of Robinson. The Chiefs and the front office stood as a team, although I am sure they were as much aware of the holes as the vociferous fans.

Even going into the home playoff game against the Peyton Manning-led Colts, there was some hope the defense would rise to the occasion. It did not, and in fact played one of its worst games of the 13-3 season. Robinson's defense was pathetic, embarrassing and totally ineffective. The 38-31 loss was as bitter as the 10-7 loss to the Colts in 1993. Only this time, instead of Linville Elliott, it was Greg Robinson who was seen as the goat and had to be driven out of town.

It was like that scene in Frankenstein when the villagers with torches in hand hunt down their tormentor and monster. It was clear Robinson had to go, and in a tearful news conference two days after the Indianapolis playoff loss, Robinson announced his resignation.

Less than two weeks later, Peterson, with Vermeil's blessing, rehired Gunther Cunningham to be defensive coordinator. Isn't it a small world? Whether this combination will finally produce Super Bowl chemistry is, as always, up for speculation. It will be debated on talk radio, in bars, on golf courses and after church.

My guess is that Carl, Dick, Al Saunders and Gunther will be bringing back the Lombardi Trophy to Kansas City in early 2005. Among those riding in the parade, I predict, will be Lamar, Hank, Lenny and I.

Will Dick Vermeil retire again if the Chiefs win a Super Bowl in 2005? I believe he will. But I'll be back. People ask me when I plan to retire. I tell them when they close the lid on the box.

The long-term future of the Chiefs in Kansas City is encouraging, even without Grigs, Vermeil, Peterson and Lamar.

Lamar's children are dedicated to this franchise staying in this city. Clark Hunt, who is Vice Chairman of the Board, has taken an active interest in sports management and will head the organization eventually. Clark, who has also been active with the soccer Wizards, is often seen in the locker room after Chiefs games. Each of Lamar's children—Sharon, Daniel, Lamar, Jr. and Clark—will form the ownership of the club, though.

Unlike the Royals' situation when Ewing and Muriel Kauffman passed away, I believe the Hunt family will hold on to this team well into this century if not the next. And I believe strongly that it will never leave Kansas City. Of course, no one in

With Clark Hunt and his beauuutiful bride, Taira.

the Hunt family will be satisfied until the Chiefs win another Super Bowl. That is the goal.

But Clark's sense of humor and style is very similar to that of his father, studious and soft-spoken. Above all, he is sensitive and alert to the rich history of Kansas City Chiefs football.

CHAPTER 12

The Sports Show

The letter is dated November 18, 1957, and is the only contract I have ever had, or required, from the Perkins family. *"In accordance with our conversation it is understood that you will handle all publicity..."* it reads in part. *"General Shows, Incorporated agrees to pay you $500 for these services...*

"Yours very truly,

Phillip D. Perkins"

I have had the honor of being with the Kansas City Sports Show for 46 of its delightful and exhilarating 50 years. Other than Fran, it is the longest-running relationship I have had in my life. Some might find that somewhat peculiar, or at the very least ironic, since I am neither a fisherman nor a hunter. Go figure.

The Show, the most popular of Kansas City's trade exhibitions, celebrated its 50th anniversary in January 2004, and like the 49 years before, filled Bartle Hall or Municipal Auditorium with outdoor enthusiasts. To put its longevity in perspective, it began as the Kansas City Boat, Sports and Travel Show when Dwight D.

Eisenhower was president and there was no Interstate 70 streaming from St. Louis to Kansas City and beyond. There was no
Chiefs, Royals or Champions Tour. Len Dawson was a high school
quarterback. George Brett still had a pacifier, and Tom Watson was
swinging plastic clubs. And if you wanted information about the
Sports Show you dialed Victor 2-0791. No need for area codes,
because they were not required for another decade or two.

I am no outdoor type, but what I love about the Sport Show
is that a great many people love the outdoors and, consequently,
love attending this annual winter extravaganza when they otherwise would be suffering from cabin fever. Never mind that I will
never be in the market for a shotgun or a trip to Montana to hunt
elk, but I absolutely love being around people who are so warm
and fuzzy about them.

And the great thing is that this show has always been a family affair, its ownership and management passed down through the
Perkins clan of Minneapolis. My first encounter with Phil Perkins
was a casual one, and at the time neither one of us would have ever
guessed the relationship would last into the next century.

It began, as with so many intimate relationships, over a drink
in a bar.

I had just returned home from Lawrence where I had been
broadcasting a KU basketball game. In order to wind down just a
little, I made a last-second decision to stop off at a neighborhood
bar near my home. How serendipitous that I ran into an old
buddy, Harry Craft, who I had known from my Joplin days. Harry
had been the Miners' manager when I had been the team's broadcaster. Harry had just been hired to replace Lou Boudreau as the
A's manager.

I sat down with Harry and another guy who turned out to be
Perkins. During our conversation, Phil explained he was a former
hockey player in the NHL and lived in Minneapolis. Naturally, I
was curious what he was doing in town since we didn't have an
NHL franchise at the time.

He was working, Perkins explained, for Nick Kahler, who
owned outdoor and travel trade shows in Minneapolis and Kansas

City. Right then and there, it was Craft who put the strong arm on Phil to hire me since I knew so much about promotion, although he had already hired a local guy, Vern Banks, to work the local media.

"Maybe you'd like to handle some of our outstate publicity," he offered.

Naturally I was interested and figured I could pick up grocery money. How fortuitous, I thought to myself, pick up an extra $100 on my way home from working the Jayhawks.

"We don't have a lot of money. Would $500 be enough?" Perkins asked.

I don't know whether he had too much to drink, or I was thinking too small, but for me to get a gig like that was like finding a couple hundred bucks in the street. It seemed like easy money, and for the first time in my life, I think, I was speechless.

In time, Kahler sold the rights to Perkins, and today Phil's son, Dave, owns the show. They are like family to me. When I first met Dave he was just a little kid hanging out with his dad. Dave Perkins is absolutely a class young man. We have all grown up with Twiggy the Squirrel, the Professor of Croaker College and the Lumberjills, a spirited all-ladies team of log jocks.

"There is nobody like Bill," Dave Perkins graciously explained to the media at the start of the 2004 Sport Show. "I believe he became a permanent fixture for the show as soon as he sat down with my dad in that bar.

"It's been a wonderful relationship. He has been everything to this show. I know he doesn't like to suggest that he is very much of an outdoorsman. But despite what he tells you, he is a pretty good shot. I remember one year, we all went down to Bubby Baier's place near Peculiar, Missouri, and Bill more than held his own with the other hunters. Grigsby has got great hand-eye coordination.

"Like everybody will tell you, the mark of Grigs is his enthusiasm. The glass is never half empty with him. It's always half full, but in Grigs's case, he wants to own the glass."

Of course, what I did in the early years was to visit all the civic clubs and promote the show coming town every January. Or visit the media. We would have a big dinner of northern pike and wild rice for the press every year prior to the show to promote all the things that would be in it. No need to do that today, though.

Before the Perkins's took over, Kahler ran things and was a real taskmaster. He could be very mean and tight. I guess he had a lot of fishhooks in his pocket.

The night before the show would open, we would have to have a dress rehearsal for all the acts that would be performing. And if Nick didn't personally like them, he had no qualms about going right up to the people involved and telling them to go to the hotel, check out and get out of town. But that was Kahler.

The Professor of Croaker College never got the hook, though. His name was Bill Steed, and he performed for a number of years, along with his frogs. His thing was a frog that lifted weights. He would have them on their backs and, yes, they would be pressing these little-bitty weights when he would rub their bellies.

One year I took a reporter from KCMO-TV, Channel 5, up to this guy's room in the Phillips Hotel so he could do a prestory. Bill's wife was the only one there and she was extremely agitated because the Professor had all his frogs loose in the bathroom. It was so embarrassing and tense, we never did get the story.

And who could forget Twiggy the Squirrel when it would get dragged all over the indoor pond on the little-bitty skis? Another guy drew big crowds because he could catch bullets in his teeth…or at least that's what we promoted. The amazing thing was not that the guy was supposed to be catching bullets with his mouth, but that people actually believed he could do it. They had the bullets marked in a certain way, and one year, a policeman even attested to him doing it! The early days reminded me of my wrestling days, because so much of it was a con job.

One year, I actually ended up in federal court because of our wrestling bear act.

All the farm boys would come to the show and want to impress their girlfriends by wrestling the bear that we had brought in for just that purpose. But what they never seemed to understand was that bear had been lying around all day and wasn't exercising the best hygiene in his cage.

But these kids would never think about that, they'd jump in the ring and by the time they got out from grappling with this bear, their girlfriends wouldn't want anything to do with them any more. I think that broke up more budding romances than anything.

One year the U.S. Department of Fish and Game brought a marshal and arrested the man and his bear because he apparently didn't have the necessary permit. The next day I had to appear in federal court with the man and his bear. Cal Hamilton was the magistrate judge. He had just finished binding over some Puerto Ricans on a murder trial and all of a sudden I show up walking down the middle aisle with a bear.

"What in the world have you gotten yourself into now, Grigsby?" he said to me that morning. The bear couldn't express himself too well, but honestly, the bear had to appear.

We have had a variety of animal acts through the run of the Sports Show. We have had wolves, mountain lions, skunks, and all kinds of waterfowl and a couple memorable snakes.

Probably the most unforgettable was a king cobra back in the late 1980s. This baby was 20 feet long and as big around as a boa, a reptile not to be taken lightly. One of the TV stations wanted to come out and do a feature on it and the guy who brought it in for the show. So I got it all arranged and we decided to do it when the snake's cage needed cleaning out. So we went into the room where the snake's cage was, and he opened its door while he was doing the TV interview. I was standing by the door watching the thing slitter toward the door and me. Well, it didn't take me very long to decide I wanted nothing to do with the cobra. Out the door I went, leaving the herpetologist and the photographer to fend for themselves. I'm no dummy.

In 2003 and 2004 we had the rattlesnake exhibit, where the fellows brought in a pile of rattlers and put them on the floor of Bartle. Talk about educational. The snakes weren't defanged, they were the real things. What was amazing is that people were able to get so close.

I like it that so many people like the outdoors, even though I have not been an active participant. I went fishing one time with Harold Ensley. We went down to Stockton Lake because he kept after me about going with him. Harold wanted to do a TV show, but the only good picture they got of me was peeing off the end of the boat. That never made it on.

But I have always enjoyed being around the show and knew all the big names who came in for it. The truth though, is that I never had the luxury of free time to go hunting and fishing like a lot of people.

And the show always seemed to create a lot of excitement much like the wrestling matches. I remember one night Mayor Roe Bartle was at the show. Roe had a tendency to sometimes fall off the wagon. One night he came in wearing his Boy Scout shorts and almost fell in the pond. He had been to an event prior to the Sport Show and had had a couple belts. I have often thought about that night when he teetered near that pond. He must have weighed 400 pounds and had he fallen into that water he would have drowned 18 people at ringside not to mention himself. The pond would have overflowed and it would have been a total disaster.

H. Roe was wonderful, and I joke about it now only because he would have. He would open that Sport Show every year because it was so good for Kansas City, and there was nothing more important to him than Kansas City.

I know it sounds like one big party, but that is hardly the case. The Sport Show is an enormous amount of work, and the Perkins family puts in a lot of effort. It is nothing to walk five miles a day down there. There are a lot of things to be done, not the least of which is trying to keep all the resort people and exhibitors happy with all their fishing tackle and gear. They're there to sell their merchandise, so it's no joke to them. It all depends on getting people through the door.

"If a problem ever arises," Perkins tells people, "Grigs can defuse anything better than anything in the world. And if Grigs

Sometimes I find myself in fast company. In this case it was racing legend A.J. Foyt.

can't do it, then his good friend and attorney, Preston Williams can. Thanks to Bill, Preston handles all of our legal issues, too."

It has been a labor of love, though. The telling thing about that I think is that everybody who works for Dave and the Sport Show stays with him. His people have been there for decades because he treats people fairly. I have never heard anyone say anything against Dave Perkins.

Over the years my role has evolved. I handle media requests but I have taken things a little more personally too. I make the rounds up and down the aisles. Sometimes I will stop at a booth when I see somebody just sitting there. I jump in and say, "Hey, let me show you how to get people over here!" So I go behind their counters and start doing a little cheerleading.

"Hey, everybody, I'm here to tell you why you should be going to Saskatoon!"

I am a cheerleader, a spokesman, and a ringmaster introducing acts and workshops, and a problem solver behind the scenes. It generally involves a 10-hour day, and over a six-day span I realistically put in close to 70 or 80 hours. But for me it's just not hard work because I like the people who I see attend every year. Now so many of those people are my friends.

The truth is I couldn't start my year without the renewal of my friendship with Dave and Harold Ensley. The three of us go back to the very roots of the Sport Show. The three of us generally covey up some time during the course of the show, and what better place than Harold's red Ford station wagon.

What a sight—and sound—to behold for anybody nearby.

"We're working on 47 years together," I quipped at this year's show.

When Harold questioned that, I couldn't resist gigging my long-time buddy.

"Hey, if it wasn't for me, you wouldn't be here anyway!"

"Yeah, yeah..." Harold said sarcastically. "How many times have I heard that?"

"I'm telling you one more time!"

I never miss an opportunity to remind The Sportsman's Friend that it was me who encouraged Harold to go into the business of promoting hunting and fishing more than 50 years ago in Joplin. It was shortly after both of us moved north that we got involved with the Sport Show and the Perkins family.

And although I am the official mouthpiece or Master of Ceremonies, any of us could qualify.

"Think about it," I pointed out in January 2004. "Perkins, Ensley, Grigsby. That's P-E-G. We're the PEG of The Sport Show!

Corny humor maybe, but I always look at life that way.

Don't misunderstand, though, Harold and I haven't had all that much to do with the success of the show. Whether we're here or not, the Kansas City Sport Show will always be a success. I only add to the show by giving it a bit of continuity for people who have been coming down for a long time.

And who knows, maybe one of these years I will get serious about fishing and hunting. I did go out duck hunting one time with my good buddies, Len Dawson, Johnny Robinson, Preston William and Eddie Bruni, who owned Gaetano's Restaurant.

We went up to Mound City to Preston's place. Like good hunters, we played cards and drank the night before. Then the next morning the alarm went off and I jumped up and demanded to know what was going on…scared to death.

"We're going out to the blind now," Preston told everybody.

"But you can't see!" I shouted back. "I'm not going out there if you can't see, we're liable to shoot each other."

Lenny and Johnny actually went, but Ed and I simply rolled over and went back to sleep. Our role was to go to Mound City, buy food and fix it for breakfast. Needless to say, I never made it to the blind. But Ed and I never got cold and wet, either. My Lord, it was cold, and who wanted to put on those big bulky waders and all?

Thank goodness, the kids never insisted I take them either fishing or hunting. Dave Perkins brought it up several times, but he is smart enough to know not to press it.

But Dave is also sharp enough to know I don't have to be an outdoorsman to be dedicated to the Sport Show. Never in my wildest dreams did I think that when his dad and I sat down for a beer that we would be forging a partnership that would last half a century.

I had no idea I would even still be alive 50 years after having that beer.

CHAPTER 13

The Family

Family has always been of central importance to Fran and me. I had two brothers, and Fran was one of eight children. It pleases me greatly that all five of our children did well in school.

Jim went on to get his Doctorate at the University of Colorado. His degree is in neuropsychology. He had a clinical practice in Boulder but gave it up to become a research scientist. He writes for medical journals and co-authored a book, *Neurodynamics of Personality*.

Paul, our left-handed bass guitarist, played with several recording groups. In the middle nineties he made a career change into the high-tech field. He has two children, Katie and John Paul, both talented musicians.

Ann, our third born, is an artist and teacher. She earned a bachelors degree from the University of Kansas and her masters from UMKC. She is married to an architect. They have two children, Sarah and Paul.

Fran and I surrounded by the family clan.

Jane, number four, attended Wichita State and the Conservatory at UMKC. She played first chair clarinet with the Chicago Civic Orchestra and was a backup in the Chicago Symphony. Today she works for a daily paper in New Jersey.

Bill, number five, got his B.S. from William Jewell. Following graduation he went off to the Peace Corps in Senegal, Africa. He lived in a thatched room hut for 2 1/2 years. Upon returning he got a Masters degree at the University of Idaho and two years later his Doctorate at Washington State. He has been on the faculty at Penn State and is currently a faculty member at Eastern Oregon University. His wife, Maria, worked for the U.N. as a microbiologist and partnered with Bill in tennis matches. They have three little ladies under 10, Esa, Giulia and Anna. Great children, all.

Of course none of this clan paid me much due when it came to my public persona. When they were just little kids they were amazed when someone asked for my autograph. They would giggle and roll their eyes when someone would recognize me.

When they were a bit older, Fran would take them to Chiefs games and they would freeze or burn up sitting by rest room heaters.

For the most part I never pushed my interests on them. They were never involved until an event in the late nineties. It seems that the boys and girls club wanted to honor Fran and me for our commitment to the community.

Charles and Patti Garney, well known for their charitable work in Kansas City, invited us to celebrate Patti's birthday and asked me to emcee the party. Their home was perfect for entertaining, with a pair of balconies overlooking the main floor. Fran and I were to stay in the room and at a prearranged signal exit to the opposite balcony and tell stories about Patty. As we walked out of the balcony, Len Dawson emerged from the opposite balcony, saying he was taking over the program when in walked all five of our children. It was a grand and surprising party.

Two weeks later—thanks to Lamar Hunt and Carl Peterson—the party moved to the Chiefs' indoor practice facility. There were friends from every corner of our lives—unions, nuns, priests, associates, friends, and folks from out of town including Merle and Jeanette Harmon, who flew in from Dallas. It was truly an unforgettable evening. Looking back I consider the success of my family our greatest accomplishment—but the kids succeeded on their own.

My children are proud of my accomplishments, perhaps, but no more than of their mother's quiet and consistent demeanor, patience and love. With our combined personalities, we sent our children on their own ways with confidence.

CHAPTER 14

Toastmaster

As soon as you become a broadcaster, you become a public speaker. It goes with the territory. You are asked to speak at all kinds of functions.

It may begin with Cub Scouts, but before long it's Boy Scouts, and then civic groups of all kinds. It is kind of like starting in the minor leagues and working your way up. That's the way it was for me in Joplin.

I started when I was 26 or 27 years old. Since then I've done about 18,000 to 20,000 speaking engagements and probably 19,000 for free. I can't remember the last time I was nervous about one of them. The only time I get nervous now is around beautiful women.

It's a great experience to do public appearances. Once you get your mind set on public speaking, you develop confidence. Confidence allows anyone to get up and speak. When I take the podium, nothing bothers me unless it's an occasional cell phone in the audience.

Once I was speaking to the Office of Emergency Management at the Lake of the Ozarks a couple years ago. Two tables from the front was a guy in a cowboy hat with a phone in his ear. I looked down while I was giving the speech and he was talking away on his cell phone.

"Excuse me, folks," I told the crowd, "I need to have a little conversation this fellow in front.

"'Hey, pardner, you with the hat on! Have I had any calls?'

"'What'd you mean?'

"'I left 'em your number.'

"'Look, I'm going to tell you something, pardner, you or that phone are going to leave here if I'm going to continue to speak.'"

The crowd got up and gave me a standing ovation.

It's important to have everyone's attention when you are speaking. I really like to work an audience. I like to make them laugh, and then make them think...or even cry maybe. It's the challenge of speaking.

Once I was in upstate New York speaking at a function. I had the audience right where I wanted them. You could have heard a whisper, I had them that quiet. And like a bullfighter, I was about to take my sword and drive it down through their shoulder blades. At that very moment of explosive silence, a waitress walked into the hall.

"We have a telephone call for Charlie Smith!" she blared out.

The spell was completely lost.

As it turned out, it was a perfect time to get her message across, at the expense of mine, of course. It blew my evening, but it turned out OK for her and Charlie.

Those things do happen.

Once I was asked to speak in Telluride, Colorado, at a rancher's convention. A thousand people were supposed to be there. I had a little time in the afternoon to take a look around the town. As I was walking back I noticed on one side of the hotel you could see lights, but on the other there were no lights whatsoever.

So I decided I'd go by the office and find out if they had a problem. They told me I'd better go get a shower in because the

I've been invited to the Indianapolis 500 numerous times and always enjoy visiting with Mary Hulman George, the chairman of the board.

power was out. It dawned on me I should find out about that night because I was supposed to speak to a group of about 500 people.

On my way down, I ran into a guy who was walking very quickly toward me.

"Are you Bill Grigsby?" he asked. "We've got a little problem."

"Your lights are out because you haven't paid your bill?" I asked.

"How'd you know?"

"All I had to do was look around," I answered.

"Well, the guy who owns the place lives out in California and he does get occasionally lazy when it comes to paying bills. He hasn't paid it for the last two months so they turned it off. Is there anything you can think of to help us get through this?"

I advised him to go into town and buy every candle he could find and then when people started showing up, to tell them they were going to have a candlelight dinner. Further I assured him I could speak loud enough to accommodate 500 people. Of course, the only thing that saved him was the fact that they still had gas to cook the food. That hadn't been turned off.

And life went on. I spoke and I'm not sure anyone ever knew the difference.

The key, as these examples illustrate, is being able to improvise and adjust as the situation dictates. Being confident is also important.

I try to get to wherever I'm speaking early so I can meet as many people as possible. If you touch flesh with them, then they're on your side. Maybe they'll laugh a little harder when the time comes if they've met you personally.

So many places, I will just stand at the door and meet all the people as they're coming in. That works well particularly if it is a farm speech. Farm folks simply just like to meet the guy who is going to be talking to them.

In any case, I never—NEVER—use notes.

What I also try to do is size up an audience in the first three or four minutes of my talk. If I can make people laugh right away I am in pretty good shape from then on. It gets the people laughing with you, or at you.

If you just get up and start firing at them like you know every-thing, they will turn against you. That hasn't happened a lot to me, but I can remember many years ago when I was doing a radio show with Hank Stram on Thursday nights during the football season. We had it at a place called U Smile, a motel where we would attract about 500 fans. The people would get out there and get gassed up good. And if the Chiefs had lost the Sunday before, they would really get on Hank. Of course, I tried to protect Hank and not let anybody go after him.

I remember one night some guy was popping off. I looked him right in the eye and let him have it.

"Who sent you over tonight, the Happy Humphrey School for Fat Heads?"

The guy got up and he was six foot eight. Later that night I was at the bar getting a drink when I heard a voice.

"Hey, I'll buy that drink."

I turned around and it was that guy. We turned out to be great friends.

I guess that's because I was mad at Hank myself, because I thought he had coached rather poorly. Before the start of the show, though, I was up at the head of the room, so he had to walk through the crowd to get in. There were some glass doors closer to where I was sitting, and sure enough Hank came in that way and was knocking on the glass for me to let him in so he wouldn't have to walk through the crowd.

I could read his lips, "OPEN THE DOOR!"

I could have opened the door, but I mouthed back to him, "But I haven't got the key." I wanted him to have to come through the crowd because I knew they were really going to go after him that night. They did, especially my six-foot-eight friends.

But I was always doing stuff like that to Hank, and thankful-ly he took it in a humorous way.

After he had gone on to New Orleans, I got a call from Hank one day.

"Bill, I'm on the Dapper Dan football banquet this year and I need a few of your stories."

"Yeah, but Henry, you always told me they weren't any good!"

"Never mind that, I need three or four of them."

So I gave him what he wanted and he seemed happy.

Funny thing, though, Wayne Larrivee, who I had worked with doing the Chiefs games for a couple years and who had gone on to Chicago, also called me and was also going to be speaking at the Dapper Dan banquet. He wanted some stories, too

"Oh, that's fine, Wayne, I can give your three or four."

I gave him the same stories I had given Hank. Fran had been in the kitchen listening to me.

"You are rotten," she told me later.

"Ok, but these guys ought to get their own material. Anyway, the fun will be in sitting back and seeing who gets to the podium first."

Later that year when I was down in Houston doing a game, Hank came into the broadcast booth.

"Hey, Hank, I haven't seen you since you did the Dapper Dan banquet, how'd it go?"

"That rotten Larrivee stole all my stories."

Neither Hank nor Wayne had any idea.

You can have fun with stuff like that.

The big annual football banquet in Kansas City is the 101, a salute to the men of professional football. It is one of the major sports dinners in the country and one of the social events of the year for our area.

For years, my good friend Bruce Rice was the master of ceremonies, and I would present one of the awards. Bruce was brilliant, as he was at all the events he would work.

In 1970 Bruce died, and they asked me if I would be the emcee, which I have been for more than 30 years now. But Bruce was the master of one-liners, and I'm more of a storyteller. That's not to say, though, that I didn't really enjoy listening to Bruce.

The 101 has changed its format to the point now, though, that you don't have a chance to express much of your personality anymore. The programs got so long that you couldn't get into the humor as much.

Lamar Hunt used to clock the program with a stopwatch. Every once in a while you would get word backstage that you were maybe 12 seconds over and you would have to speed it up. Lamar is a stickler for perfection. He wants things done right, and I understand that.

Then we would get toward the end, and Lamar would take longer than he should. Hank Stram would sometimes never get off. Mike Ditka got in the sauce one time and he almost had to be pulled away from the podium. But you just cannot control the other speakers. You tell them they've got three minutes, but it doesn't mean they'll hold it to three minutes. People get to talking about their life and they want to thank Aunt Tilley and cousin Bertha.

It's that way when you attend political gatherings where there are 15 politicians. Each of them is allotted two minutes and each takes 15. I've gotten to the podium at some of those functions at midnight, and there's nobody left to listen. I'll look around and there's a guy sitting at the head table. I'll thank him for staying and listening, and he'll tell me he didn't have any choice, he's the next speaker. I use that story when I want to needle somebody for taking too much time.

I'll never forget the first year I did the 101 after Bruce Rice died. I was walking up to the podium and some woman grabbed my arm as I was walking by her.

"You've got big shoes to fill."

"I know, but we wore the same size."

The thing is that when you're in this business, you can't be too thin-skinned. I learned that when I was broadcasting major league baseball. The letters you get from people who don't even know you rip into you pretty good. That's just human nature. That's another reason to meet as many people as possible before you speak. The more people you introduce yourself to, the better chance that they'll like you.

Through the years, though, I haven't experienced many flops. But the fact is that there are times when you feel you've done a great job, and times when you feel you haven't. And sometimes there are just dead crowds.

What I have refused to do since I started, though, was to get into any "blue" material. There are stories you can tell in sports that are borderline that you can use without embarrassing yourself or someone else. What always bothered me when people started to tell "blue" jokes were the women and children in the audience. It's the same thing when you go to a movie and you hear filthy material. I just don't feel comfortable sitting there with my wife when they throw that stuff in your face. Call me old school, I guess. But I just don't know what's funny about that kind of stuff. It's for shock value, I think.

I get razzed some about telling some of my favorite stories over and over. But what I have learned in public speaking is that if you tell stories well, you can tell them over and over. I have people beg me to tell them stories that I've told at other gatherings and events. People love to hear the stories of the old Chiefs.

One of the favorites is the time Hank Stram and I were invited up to Fort Leavenworth to speak at the Command Staff School. They asked me to speak and bring Hank along. This was in 1964 when we both were on short grass and not making much money.

I went to Hank and said, "Henry, you wanna go with me to speak to the colonels?"

"What are they paying?" he asked me.

"I have no idea, but whatever they give us is more than we've got."

So we go up there, Hank is on the program first and I know he'll talk for an hour. And while he is up there, the general comes by and gives me an envelope.

"Bill, here's your money," he tells me. "Thanks for coming up."

After he hands me the envelope, I decide to go back and see how much we've got. I've got the little ones at home and need the money, but I've got to split it with Hank. So I go back to the toilet and open the envelope. Four $100 bills fall out. Now remember, back in 1964 that was a pretty good jackpot.

I think to myself that's really too much, so I take one of the four bills and stick it in my pocket, put the other three hundred back in the envelope and seal it back up.

Just about that time, Hank is coming off the podium and as I'm passing him on the steps he bends over and asks me in a whisper, "What'd ya find out about the money?"

"Here, the general gave me the envelope, it's all sealed up and I don't know what's in it."

"Give me that!"

So I turn the envelope over to him, and I begin my talk.

That night as we're driving back to Kansas City I asked him how we had done.

"I was great, you were rotten," he growls.

"I don't mean that, how much money did we get?" I ask him.

"Those tight bastards, they only gave us $200!" he snaps.

He loves the story himself. I've probably told the story 300 times, but people still howl in laughter. It has never failed to get a laugh. I could tell it and retell it four times a night and still get a laugh.

I've got a file of stories at home that I can draw upon. In fact, some of the paper is getting a bit tattered I've had them so long. But I don't need the file, because I've got it all up in my brain anyway.

Dianne Stafford, a reporter for *The Kansas City Star*, wrote a column one time about the ability to tell stories. She wrote that locally, Bill Grigsby is a great storyteller and sometimes will even tell the truth.

When I get a request now, I don't even really prepare. I quit doing that when I was invited to speak down in Bartlesville, Oklahoma, at a convention of women. I went down there because it was a paying job, and the women who hired me said I would be speaking to women 30 to 60 years of age. I thought about it and planned what I might tell this age group. But when I got down there and looked around the room, it was more like a 60-to-90 age group. So had I spent a lot of time preparing, it would have been useless.

Just before I began, the woman who had organized the convention wanted a copy of my speech. I told her I didn't have one. Then she wanted the title. I told her I didn't have one.

"Well, there's a reporter over here that wanted a copy," she barked at me. "And you don't even have a title?"

"No. But if you really want to know the truth, it's a surprise."

Frankly, it was going to be a surprise to me, too, because I had to disregard what I was going to deliver because it wasn't pertinent anymore. So I sat down at the head table at dinner and noticed there was a little advertisement on the table about making keys and locks there in Bartlesville. So it struck me, I should talk about the keys to life we all look for.

So I talked for 30 brilliant minutes about the keys to opening doors in your life. But at the end, I gave them one final message.

"But, really ladies, when you break it all down, isn't it true that the one key that we're all looking for is the key to the Kingdom!"

I got a standing ovation. The organizer rushed over and said I had done it; I had really surprised her.

But when I speak to any group, I do put my feelings into it. As a result, I can normally hold an audience pretty well because I do speak from my heart, although you almost always have to have some humor in it, too.

I learned a long time ago that if you have a 30-minute speech and you can get them to laugh for 20 minutes, you can get them to listen to your real message for 10 minutes. It's a formula that I've worked out in my mind. I can get up and speak without even looking at a clock and speak 30 minutes exactly. I think that's because of the broadcasting experience.

I've also done eulogies and funerals, although I'm not real crazy about doing them. That's especially true if the recently departed is a dear friend. One of the ones I did last year, the widow asked me if I would make people laugh. And as she wished, I had everyone laughing at the funeral.

But I don't have a problem with that, because if a person has lived a long and good life, death is not a terrible thing, and funerals can be a celebration. When Ed Sheppard, our engineer on the A's broadcasts, died, we all treated it like a roast. We all got up and told funny stories about Ed, who was like a brother to me. It turned out to be a beautiful experience. That's exactly the kind of funeral I would like for myself. Maybe I'll tape record it for everybody else and let them play it while everybody is drinking.

Once I had to do something of a drive-by eulogy. I had gone to the Hi-Point Hunting Club near Breckenridge, Missouri with Whitey Herzog and some other friends for a pheasant hunt. And since I don't do much hunting, but like to be around the guys who do like to hunt, I spent most of my time back at the clubhouse with owner Al Guffey and his son, Brian.

During the afternoon, one of the guys in our party, Dr. Jim Lanning, had been stricken with a heart attack and died while in the field. And although Dr. Lanning had died in the pursuit of doing something he truly loved, upland bird hunting, everybody else understandably was rather traumatized by his sudden death.

After the ambulance took Dr. Lanning out of the field, everybody gathered back at the clubhouse and was stumbling around in shocked disbelief. That's when I got everybody gathered round in a circle. We grasped each other's hands, and I provided a little prayer that seemed to bring everyone peace.

And believe it or not, I have turned down some speaking engagements, too.

One day I was asked to speak at a gathering of about 800 judges and lawyers. I asked them what the fee was, and they told me I would have a great dinner and a fun evening.

"I have that at home every night," I told them.

Wasn't it interesting that they expected to be paid for their time, but they weren't willing to pay a speaker!

When it comes to conventions or groups like that, I expect to be paid. They're professionals and I am a professional. But when it comes to a charity or a nursing home, I don't expect to be paid.

And I don't alter my enthusiasm or energy for a group whether it is two or two hundred, or whether I am being paid an honorarium or not. If people have come to hear you speak about something, it is important to respect them and treat them well regardless of the number. When I was with Mark Twain Bank, I would invite someone like Joyce Hall, the founder of Hallmark Cards, or another big name in Kansas City to speak. They would wonder why they were being invited down there and I would end up with people from all walks of life at one of the tables. I even had people as far away as Istanbul, Turkey. I would introduce each one of them, and talk about them. I would make each one of them important. They would love it. I learned this in radio, because if you think about it, you are just talking to that one microphone.

CHAPTER 15

The Unforgettables

I have friends whom I have known more than 60 years and some I have had for six minutes. I find it very easy to meet and enjoy people, most of whom want to wish you well.

That was never so evident to me than after I had my heart attack. At my first public appearance at the Chiefs football game and a month later at the 50th anniversary of the *Kansas City Sports Show*, people were very warm. There was very much a heartfelt love that I experienced from longtime friends and those new faces that I bumped into.

"Bill's energy level hasn't dropped after all these years," Gary Coleman, general manager of the Chiefs Radio Network told a friend. "He's always positive and an inspiration to those around him. He keeps me hopping. His passion is limitless."

There have been so many friends in my life's orbit, so many unforgettable personalities. Some have already been mentioned in these pages, some you are very familiar with, like Len Dawson, Lamar Hunt or Carl Peterson. But some are, perhaps, just as close but not as well known. Like my good friends Preston Williams, Jim Allen, Jim Watson and Dave Broderick, Mr. Augusta.

Having grown up poor and hustling, you learn a lot about life and about people. You learn how to treat people and how to get along with all kinds of people from every walk of life. I have never paid much attention to a person's economic wealth, their religion or the color of their skin.

But remember, those of us who are in the public eye are generally very busy and often have difficulty finding good, quality time with others because we're on a treadmill of sorts. You never have enough time to spend with friends as you'd like to. It's just the way it works. That can often make it tougher on your family. Fran sometimes gets short-changed waiting for me to wrap up a luncheon, banquet or some other charitable event I might be involved in.

There have been so many colorful characters, so many stories. And except for maybe Charlie Finley, there is nobody I haven't thoroughly enjoyed, and hopefully most have enjoyed my company. That's not to say I haven't had my share of verbal wrestling matches.

Let me give you a little insight into some of more unforgettables whom I have crossed paths with.

Tom Watson—I have known Kansas City's premier golfer for more than 30 years. I first came across him when I used to play the Kansas City Country Club with a couple buddies. He was just another good young player who had potential. Stan Thirsk, who I played with occasionally, bragged about him a lot and was Tom's early mentor.

Hank Stram—Henry was a real character. He was very much like Frank Sinatra in that Hank did it his way. We had a great deal of fun needling each other constantly.

Archie Moore—One of boxing's greatest names. Came into prominence when segregation was very much a way of life. But Archie, who was black, never complained or let it affect him in any adverse way. One of the greatest competitors I have ever known. Pulled himself out of the ghetto and made something of his life. I have always looked at Archie as a champion for that instead of his boxing titles.

Joe Louis—My favorite athlete of all time. I'll never forget 1936 when he fought Max Schmeling. I was at a Y camp down in the Ozarks and walked about 10 miles so I could hear it on the radio. I cried all the way home because Joe got knocked out. He was my hero, and I've been to his grave at Arlington several times.

George Brett—Known him for a long time and spent lots of time with him. George was born—like all great players—to be a baseball player. He was a born winner in much the same way Ted Williams was. There are lots of journeymen ball players, but George is in an elite category that very few ever get to. When George was young he could be ornery. But above all else, he was one hell of a baseball player, you could see it in his eyes. He was like a wild mustang, but he became refined and is now a wonderful husband and father. He's been a Godsend for Kansas City.

Whitey Herzog—Wasn't an outstanding player, but a great manager, much like Dick Williams, who managed the A's. Both were journeymen ball players, but became stars in the managerial ranks. They were very much students of the game and made that their advantage once they were finished playing. Both should be in the baseball Hall of Fame. They were a bit of wildmen, too. But then again, baseball, because you play so many games, is different than most sports. You have to learn how to blow off steam.

Mickey Mantle—Absolutely a wild stallion. When he first came to Joplin he was fresh off the farm and he definitely was in a mood to test life. He was very much like Brett, pure baseball. And like George, it was obvious to everybody that the kid had amazing ability. As time went along, though, Mick could get testy and not be the nicest guy in the world. He sometimes could be mean to everybody…little kids or senior citizens. I think New York City did that to him to a large degree. I know he got very tired of signing the autographs. How do you describe Mickey? All everything!

Frank Lane—The A's general manager under Charlie Finley. He knew every stripper in America. He scouted strippers and ball players at the same time down in South America. He was always getting phone calls at the hotel. One time when he worked in Chicago for the Comiskey family, Mrs. Comiskey looked down one time before a game and there was Frank with a flame-throwing stripper and Mrs. Comiskey got quite upset about it.

Hank Bauer—A good buddy of mine. Another two-fisted man who had been a Marine. If you were in a barroom brawl you wanted to look around and see Hank on your side. He was a tough-minded player and another one of those guys who went on to become a pretty good manager although the teams he had weren't all that good. Finley fired him three times before it was over. I asked him once why he would ever go back with Finley. "I needed the money," was his reply. Did I also say Hank was very honest? A few times when Hank would get wind that Finley was going to fire him he would call his own news conference first and quit just to take the wind out of Charlie's sails.

Billy Martin—Probably the poster child for the bad-boy ball players. He was a whiskey-drinking, good player. But he was just a little crazy, more so than any of the others of that era. He always wanted to do things his way, and it constantly got him into trouble. When you get paired up with people like Steinbrenner, a guy like Billy is going to come out the loser.

Bill Veeck—I had the privilege of getting to know the guy pretty well. He had been around a lot, and I met him before he started running the Chicago White Sox. I first met him in St. Louis. Just to be around Veeck was to be around an exciting person. A product of World War II, he got jungle rot in Panama, smoked a lot and ended up losing a leg. He had an ashtray built into his artificial leg. He would simply pull up his pant legs and dump the ashes in his knee. Once when I and Joe McGuff, sports editor of *The Kansas City Star*, were in Boston, all of us went to a bar for a couple drinks. After about four hours of drinking, Veeck pulled off his artificial leg and started banging it on the floor, rattling the windows in the place. He was a born showman. Of course everybody knows about the story of Eddie Gaedel, the midget he signed to play baseball. He wanted to put people in the stadiums. He started out in St. Louis, went to Cleveland and finally to

Chicago. He used to have all kinds of promotions, where bartenders would get in free one night and nurses the next. Sometimes he would have promotions where he would give away 1,000 pounds of potatoes. And if you won, brother, they were yours and you had to get them home somehow.

Roger Maris—One night he and I and Nellie Fox were in an after-hours joint until the wee hours of the morning. The next day it was about 108 degrees at Comiskey Park and Roger was apparently totally unaffected, because he hit two home runs that day. Roger was a quiet type, unlike a lot of players back then. But Roger would have a few now and then, let's put it that way. He was a born Yankee and was cheated out of the home run record by a stubborn commissioner.

Buck O'Neil—An old soldier. To be with Buck is a glorious experience when he starts talking about the early days of Negro baseball. He told me once about a tournament they played in Denver. The only way they could get there was to ride the rails in boxcars. There was a detective who worked for one of the railroad lines who was a mean son of a bitch so they would always have to get off at a stop out in western Kansas to avoid the guy. They would then hop another freight train just to avoid him. But even today there's absolutely no bitterness in Buck that he was denied so much because he was a black man.

Jim Colbert—Another one of this area's great golfers, who came out of K-State. I worked with Jim on raising money to fight cystic fibrosis. He is a great champion for that. Always gracious, always willing to do whatever you asked of him and always a friend and winner.

Joe Montana—Very fun to be around. And what I remember foremost about Joe is that he never, ever tried to overwhelm you with his greatness. He always tried to downplay his accomplishments and play up his regular-guy personality. Most times he was sort of quiet, but if you got him in a group he could get pretty animated. I remember one bar up in Wisconsin during training camp where he would get real mad because a lot of the women in the bar would come up and pinch his ass. You could tell it bothered him a lot. When he was quarterbacking the Chiefs and we were on road trips sometimes we would have to stop the bus away from the front door of the hotel, so he could go in the back door to avoid all the women waiting for us. In 40 some years of broadcasting I don't think I ever saw anyone who could bring a team back in the closing minutes like Joe could. Len Dawson was close.

Len Dawson—Of all the athletes I have been around—whether it be football, baseball, boxing or whatever—Len had the greatest heart as a competitor. And I was around some of the greats—Mantle, Maris, Montana, Chamberlain. Dawson couldn't match them physically. He was not big and strong. But it was Dawson who never accepted or understood the meaning of defeat. He might have used 10,000 other not-so-nice words, but never defeat. He had the heart, but maybe not the body, of say a Trent Green of today. The closest Lenny ever got to weights was to simply look at them. I call him Leonardo, because of his artistry in football. He also was one of the most respected athletes by the other players. And what I liked the most is that after every Chiefs game, win or lose, I never heard him utter a word of criticism toward a teammate. He never did. Len was the greatest athlete I ever saw.

Marcus Allen—A guy who had a reputation of being sort of quiet and reclusive. But he was relaxed and very easy to talk to. For the most part, though, he was always business in the locker room and wouldn't sit around and small talk. Probably the best ever at getting you five yards when you absolutely had to have five yards. He could smell the end zone like nobody I've have ever seen. And if the Chiefs lost, it was hard for him to accept and shrug it off back in the locker room. The players who always worried me a little bit were the ones who were laughing after a loss back in the locker room. He wasn't that kind.

Dan Devine—I was the master of ceremonies for his retirement party that celebrated his careers at MU, Notre Dame and Green Bay. People from all three of those institutions were there at the Fairmont Hotel on the Plaza. The program went on and on and on. Everybody who spoke thought his or her story of Dan was better than anybody else's. The thing started at six o'clock and I felt so sorry for Dan and his wife, who was in a wheelchair at the time. As it turned out the whole thing was like the Battle of the Bulge. Finally at about five minutes to midnight, it was Dan's turn to get up and respond to the whole evening. Just before he got up, I turned to him and whispered in his ear, "Dan, can you cut your remarks a little bit short? If you don't I'm going to have to pay another day's rent on this damn tux." He just laughed and laughed. "Bill, after this I'm going to just say 'Thanks' and we're all going to get out of here." Even still, we didn't finish until one o'clock. It was murder. Dan Devine was a brilliant coach, but he didn't talk very much.

Norm Stewart—Another great MU coach and very much a dear friend. One of the all-time most colorful men I've known as a player, coach and individual. But a guy who tempered himself as he got older and wiser. He learned a lot about people as he aged and was one of those people who enjoyed MU basketball the longer he was there. He was certainly one of the all-time greatest athletic figures in Missouri sports history. And people began to like him more as he went on. That was evident when he would go over to Lawrence to play KU, where he became a favorite of the fans. That's very hard to do when you're an MU coach.

Phog Allen—I had a lot of great quality time with Phog and really liked the man. When we went on road trips, it would either be by train or slow plane, so we spent a lot of time together, especially when we would make the west coast trips from Washington state on down. Phog, Max Falkenstein and I would always have breakfast together and it would turn into quite a session. I called Max "The Fox" and he called me "The Cap" because I always wore a cap. Phog was very controversial and always lambasting the Amateur Athletic Union. He hated the AAU and didn't have any problem letting people know it. Phog also had a great many theories about basketball and how it needed to be changed. He was a strong advocate of raising the basket. I can only imagine what he would think if he were around today and saw the size of today's players. One of his favorite sayings was that Dr. Naismith invented this game as one of skill, not shooting from a distance. Phog was always trying to figure out ways to get crosswise with the press. And he was every bit as large as his legend. He was a brilliant man who would get so wrapped up in the game that he would forget who his players were...literally. He spoke all over the country about basketball and never had much of a life off the court. One day I was getting a haircut over in Brookside and the barber asked me what I had thought of the KU game the night before that I had broadcast, and I told him I thought Phog was nuttier than a fruit-cake for the way he coached. Well, all of a sudden the little boy in the chair next to me spun around and proclaimed proudly, "Hey, that's my granddad!" Both the grandson and Phog's son just laughed, because they were used to those kinds of comments. But there is no questioning his greatness, he was probably the greatest of all KU coaches. Phog, in all, coached 48 years and brought KU a national title in 1952. He coached the Jayhawks for 37 years, and overall won 746 games. He was also an osteopathic doctor and treated such people as Mickey Mantle and Ted Williams during his medical practice.

Roy Williams—Another one of KU's all-time great basketball coaches. Most of my involvement with Roy, though, was in the golf celebrity business. I was always getting him to come over to play in one of the skins' games to help raise money for something. He and George Brett loved to play together with some of the Champions Tour players. I have a great deal of admiration for Roy, professional and personal. And, boy, did he like playing golf, even though he was a little intimidated by some of the crowds that came to watch him. He mentioned one time in a pregame show with Max that my broadcast of the Final Four in 1954 when he was 10 years old was one of the most exciting he had ever heard. He had been listening to it in North Carolina and it was one of the reasons he had become interested in the game. That made me feel very good, to know that one of the great minds of the game would say something like that. I know a lot of people were bitter when he left KU for North Carolina, but I think it was a very good thing for Roy. He put in a nice career in Lawrence, and I think it was about time for him to revitalize himself. I don't know what it is exactly, but something goes stale with coaches once they've been somewhere 10 years or so. It happened with Hank Stram and Marty Schottenheimer, who both started going downhill.

Cotton Fitzsimmons—The ultimate in fun coaches. He was a blast at K State and just as much or even more fun when he came to coach the Kansas City Kings of the NBA. And I got to know him even better when he went to Arizona to coach the Phoenix Suns. I would go out there to play golf with him. He's certainly not your normal, run-of-the-mill coach. Very sharp, very animated. He and his wife, Joanne, are just lovely, lovely people who would do anything for you. Without question, Cotton is one of the very best basketball coaches ever. Great basketball mind. But then again, Cotton would have been a success at anything he did because of enthusiasm. What an ornery sense of humor. He's kind of a little leprechaun.

Ollie Gates—I've known the guy forever. I admire him greatly because he's someone who looks beyond himself. He has had good fortune, but only because of a lot of hard work. Ollie Gates is one of the hardest-working businessmen I have ever had the privilege of knowing. He is a lot like a football or basketball coach. He demands perfection from the people who work for him. That's the main reason the Gates name is so tied to success. A lot of times he would call and say, "Get in the car with me, we've got a trip to make." We would go over to the east side of Kansas City and he would show me areas of blight, children with little hope in their eyes and he would demand that we together would have to do something about it. And he has done something about it. He used his own money to help those little kids. And he's done it without much fanfare simply because he felt compelled. He's changed the personality along Paseo and 12th Street. He has been a motivating force in upgrading the quality of life for people. He created a group once called Enshriners. He got Jack Bush, Buck O'Neal, Otis Taylor, Bubble Klice...a group of black sports figures and coaches. They were a group of black men dedicated to doing things for the kids of Kansas City. He asked me to be a part of it—

Good buddies, me and Ollie Gates.

I was one of only white men to be asked—and I consider it one of the greatest privileges of my life to be a part of the Enshriners. We still meet once a month. Most people in Kansas City know nothing of the group.

H. Roe Bartle—Bigger than life. And very much a Jekyll and Hyde in many ways. He was big in Boy Scouts, and he would tromp around in his shorts, which was kind of weird, I thought, because he weighed about 300 pounds. With his bellowing voice, he probably made more friends for Kansas City throughout the United States than anybody in history. People loved him, and he was probably the best public speaker I have ever known. I leaned some tricks from Roe. He told he how to overcome the problem of forgetting people's names. He gave me some word association games to play. A couple weeks later I was introduced to a woman by the name of O'Hare, so I remembered her name because she had nice-looking hair. Some time after I met her, Fran and I were at a party and saw her there. When I introduced her to Fran I said,

"Honey, I'd like you to meet Kathleen O'Rear." I guess it was more than her hair I remembered. I was lucky because Fran and Kathleen O'Hare just laughed. Now, when I can't remember someone's name, I just refer to him or her as "old pardner."

Marilyn Maye—One of my old buddies from way back. A great entertainer. She is from Kansas City but someone who could play anywhere. She was on Johnny Carson a lot and for good reason. She is a beautiful talent. She spent a lot of time rooting for the Chiefs in the early days. One of my favorite photos is one with me, Tony DiPardo, Marilyn and Warpaint. Very much a champion of Kansas City, she is one class lady. She sent me a lovely note in March of 2001: "Dear Bill, Too much time has gone by since the December Rockhurst show, forgive me. I want you to know how much I appreciate you being there! As always, you're The Master in front of an audience and it was an honor for me that you came to do the introduction. So much time goes by between our meetings and it's always a joy to pick up right where we left off. That's true friendship. Thanks for being a true friend. Cheers & Hugs, Marilyn."

Stuart Symington—Missouri's legendary democratic senator for many years. He had presidential stature. The man was quality, and he served when people truly respected their elected officials. He headed up the Air Force when I first met him, and then I worked with him when he went to Washington D.C. I introduced him at many gatherings, and I did so because I liked how he carried himself and how he represented Missouri. Quality, quality, quality is the simple way to described him.

Bill Morris—Very hard-working lt. governor who got a lot of stuff done in the back room. And that's the way you had to do it back then. Too bad it doesn't work so much now and that partisan politics has taken hold so much. Morris cared greatly for the people of Missouri. Politics has changed so much. It used to be that it took a handful of people to really accomplish things, and Bill was that kind of guy who could get people together to make something happen. People like Gov. Hearnes, Sam Long, Jack Steadman, Emanuel Clever and Dick Berkley.

Anita Gorman—I don't think there is anyone who can get things done better than Anita. We worked on the Fireman's Memorial together. She is a dynamo. She was the first women selected to the Park Board and the first woman selected to the Missouri Conservation Commission. No one in Kansas City can get more community support for a project than she can. She gets things done, much needed things. A lot of things are planned for years, but don't get done until Anita gets involved. If you get Anita behind something, it will be done.

Howard Cosell—A pompous bore. Everybody I ever knew was always a little uncomfortable and embarrassed to be around him. He was very much the same kind of opinionated person off the air as on. In Howard's defense, though, he was not paid to be fair, just interesting. He was that, and he occasionally had something good to say about Kansas City. He was here in the late seventies to do the Royals and Boston Red Sox games for ABC. It was blacked out here in Kansas City, but Cosell did have some nice things to say for once. "We're at Royals Stadium in Kansas City, and there is none more beautiful," he told the national audience during the fourth inning. "But the whole complex here, I think, is the best in the country, with Arrowhead Stadium." Whitey Herzog was the manager then, and Howard praised the White Rat. "He's been through this before, and they always seem to come on strong around August. He is a colorful guy who has taken a lot of heat here. He was booed unmercifully yesterday."

Ewing Kauffman—He's gone, but the memory of Ewing stays with anyone who knew him. He liked action on the golf course, at a gin table or at Marion Labs. His generosity gave hope to many young people. He brought back the excitement of Major League Baseball in Kansas City. The world needs more people like Ewing.

Ray Zakovitz—I met Ray when he was in the Secret Service detail with President John Kennedy in Florida. The Kansas City Athletics were in training at West Palm Beach and the Kennedy clan was in nearby Palm Beach. After his retirement from government, he and his family settled in Kansas City where he is still heavily involved in law enforcement and community activities. Ray is a one-of-a-kind individual.

Del Dunmire—He made one mistake early in life and he has paid it back ten-thousand fold since the day he screwed up a bank robbery—simply because he needed money and thought a bank was the best source. He has given over two and a half million dollars to law agencies to assist in crime prevention. And his gifts to the needy run into the millions. He is a very smart and talented person who has fun with his wealth.

Dennis Watley—Dennis came aboard 14 years ago and his expertise has led the Chiefs to attendance records every year. He is Senior VP of the Chiefs sales, marketing, advertising, promotions development and stadium operations and fulfills the same postions for the Wizards soccer team. Commissioner Paul Tagliabue said the Chiefs have the best production and fan atmosphere in the NFL.

Dick Berkley—His terms as mayor of Kansas City will be remembered as years of substantial growth. Alhtough a Republican, Dick served the people with equal enthusiasm. He numbered people from all walks of life as his friends. He still gives Kansas City his best shot.

Charles Wheeler—He went from mayor to state senator with stops in between as a champion of Kansas City. The downtown air terminal bears his name. He is worthy of any award. A true servant of the people.

John Q. Hammons—One of the great visionaries. At 83 he hits the office at five in the morning and leaves at six in the evening. Springfield, Missouri's No. 1 cititzen. One of the nation's largest hotel builders and owners. Established the Missouri Sports Hall of Fame and paid for it. Has major investments in the area include Tiffany Springs Development.

The Chiefs of the Sixties—Talk about unforgettable people, these replants from Texas will always be a part of our lives. Many who made the trip north still remain in our town. Otis Taylor, Len Dawson, Fred Arbanas, Bobby Bell, Buck Buchanan, Bobby Ply, Ed Budde—and a bit later, Jim Lynch, Walter White, Larry

Marshall, Curtis McClinton and Jan Stenerud. Arbanas made it afterward in the political arena, Dawson in TV and the others found success in the business field. To a man they all credited Hank Stram, their mentor, with having a tremendous influence on their lives.

Jack Steadman—Chairman of the board. Right hand of Lamar from the teams of Texas to today. Jack served the Chiefs in every major front office position until he moved to chairman when Carl Peterson came aboard. Jack is one of the orginal Chiefs.

Denny Thum—Denny joined the team 30 years ago. His niche has been on the contract side. And today he is recognized the league over for his front-office magic in the area of salary caps and his ability to assist Peterson in the contract negotiations. He has a bright future in the NFL.

Watson and Allen—Jim Watson and Jim Allen are late entries into the Unforgettable Hall of Special People. I met the pair six years ago. We struck a chord. I was coming off 22 years of working at a bank. How about joining them at the beautiful new National Golf Club? It did not take long to make that decision. Here were two energetic guys with a dream—it couldn't miss. And predictably it has become a total success. And they even threw in a fancy new Parkville Commons Center with a Community Center and major shopping amenities.

Joe McGuff—A true friend and gentleman. Joe's integrity was his mark as a sports reporter, editor and publisher. He is currently fighting off the ravages of ALS. Still able to come up with a ready smile—his illness has not affected his ability to think and write those thoughts. Kay is his guiding light—the kids are his dreams. I love the guy.

Harold Ensley—The Fisherman's Friend has turned a sinker and a tiny tot into a lifetime of fun, excitement and a very good financial position. I met him in Joplin in my early days of radio, and 50-some years later we are still friends—make that good friends. Harold has traveled to every corner of the globe—and only injury and a weary body have kept him close to home. His wonderful kids will carry on the fishing mystique and name.

Dave Perkins—Dave's dad brought the biggest trade show featuring fishing and hunting equipment to our town 50 years ago—and after his passing, son Dave has thrilled millions of Midwesterners with the great outdoors that comes indoors. Dave takes this spectacular event to Des Moines and Minneapolis—and, of course, Bartle Hall in Kansas City. He has changed the winter mindset—and turned a dull, cold winter into visions of fun.

Stan Thirsk, Bud Williamson and Charlie Lewis—Three of Kansas City's top golf professionals. Evidence of their quality is the fact that all three spent most of their grown life at the Kansas City Country Club, Blue Hills Country Club and Mission Hills. All outstanding golfers and teachers—and all portrayed the class of what the PGA is all about.

The Departed—Stone Johnson, Mack Lee Hill, Jerry Mays, Aaron Brown, Buck Buchanan, Reg Carolan, George Daney, Jim Tyrer, Derrick Thomas, Joe Delaney and Tommy O'Boyle, long-time coach and friend.

CHAPTER 16

Contributions

I f there is anything I have tried to be in this life, it is involved. More than anything I have wanted to contribute.

I have never had what some might consider one full-time job that required I work nine to five. There is no 25-year anniversary Wittnauer on my wrist. My loyalties have been to people rather than to the security of full-time employment. That is not to say I haven't been extremely loyal to those organizations in which I have put in my time. But more to the point, I have been loyal to the idea of serving the people who are served by those institutions.

Added together, I have had more than 40 jobs in my life. I have sold manure, Oldsmobiles, cucumbers, insurance, gutters, pro wrestling, bank loans, booze and beer. But I have also made pitches for baseball, football and basketball, America and God. I have advocated for victims' rights, the working class, the poor and elderly.

Sports are not my entire agenda. I like art, music and even write a little. I write country and western music and got a check recently for one of my tunes. But I like to do everything.

People perhaps know me best as a sports broadcaster, but how many know that I once served as a deputy marshal in transporting a dangerous criminal?

There are those who claim I am the consummate politician. I take that as a compliment, even in today's contentious political climate. Maybe I should have run for office, certainly I had my opportunities and, I believe, a flair for it.

I got actively involved in politics when I got into the beer business. I got to know Senator Stuart Symington. Every one of the governors I helped. Maybe because they could always use me. I would be called on to introduce them at many of their public speaking events. That came from my wrestling background.

"Ladies and gentlemen, let me introduce a man who has dedicated his life to us," I would begin at political functions. They loved to hear that, those politicians.

The politics thing got to be real serious in the mid-1960s to late '60s. I was doing the Chiefs and we were having success. And the head of Armco Steel took a liking to me and gave me a lot of encouragement to make a run.

Bill Hull was the U.S. congressman from the district at the time, but he was retiring so I had a lot of support to take his seat in Congress. I had a lot of support from the Democrats and the unions to go for it. I was all pumped up. Fran and I talked about it quite a bit, and at one point I told her I was going to do it. She was pretty clear about her wishes. She told me when I filed, she would file. Only she was not talking about public office. Fran has tolerated a lot in our lives, but she wouldn't tolerate that.

It was hard raising the kids. And let me put it this way, SHE had been raising them. And if you recall, the '60s was a time of revolt for young people. We saw families all around us falling apart because of kids rejecting their families' values. The kids were playing one against the other.

I guess I was intrigued by politics, because to me politics was just another version of pro wrestling. I hope I am not bragging, but I think I would have really been good at it. I know how to play the bullshit game. And I can be a very dynamic speaker, especially if I believe in the cause. I can be forceful in the way I believe in people and issues. Even now I think of that pivotal time when I was considering it and wonder how far it could have gone.

Fran was not in favor of my entry into politics, but banking was OK. I suppose that is because it did not take me away to Washington—maybe a lot of other places but not for an extended period of time certainly.

I got involved in banking originally through Interstate Securities, who I was doing some part-time PR work for, and Charlie Aylward. Charlie came from an old banking family. They had the bank down at ninth and Walnut and they wanted me to come in and represent them in the early 1980s.

Until that point I really had no experience in banking, other than borrowing money from banks. But most of all they wanted me out in the public helping to sell the place. I worked with them down there and did a good job, I think.

The bank eventually became Centerre and they had a branch out of the Plaza, where I ended up. One day a week, the banking business was conducted on the golf course for me. It was part of the PR end of the job. Every Thursday at noon I would run across the street, jump in the car and hurry out to the course. We parked in one of those garages where you left your keys in the ignition.

So one day, I dashed out of the office, into the garage and out to the course. When I got there, one of the guys said to hurry up, we were on the tee.

As I walked by the back seat I looked in and there was some racquetball equipment, which made me wonder when I had started playing racquetball. As I looked at the car I realized I didn't have my car...but then again all General Motor cars look alike. It was somebody else's car.

At that point, I had to go over to my foursome and tell them I had just stolen a car and had to rush it back to the Plaza. Later I found out that the guy who owned the car was a prominent attorney. I was lucky he never knew what had happened.

I was hired by Mark Twain Bank mostly to do public speaking and networking…putting people together for a greater good. That is how I met and worked with a man named Sam Long. I was working at the bank when someone called and said, "Bill, there's a fellow by the name of Sam Long who needs your help. Sam is the head of the operating engineers and needs some fine-tuning. He needs to have somebody work with him on his speaking abilities. He's pretty rough and he's moving up in the union ranks and getting into some heavy responsibilities and he needs somebody like you who can sit down with him and work with him."

So Sam, who had a lot of union money in Mark Twain Bank, and I met. What I found was a guy who was the business manager and president of Local 101 but whose every other word was a bleeper. I mean he was rough. ROUGH. The first thing he told me when I sat down in his office was to be careful because his office could be wired. At that point I was worried about what I had actually gotten into. He told me when you are in the union business that everybody in the federal government wants to know what you are up to. Only he did not say it so nicely. So I was very blunt and honest with him, and told him he was going to be a real challenge. It was a lot like *My Fair Lady*.

So we went to work trying to break him of the constant swearing. But amazingly, he was a willing student and he listened to me. As a result, I developed a great rapport and friendship with the man.

In some ways our backgrounds were similar. We had both grown up survivors. He had grown up tough, coming out of the north end of Kansas City. He had to fight his way to school and fight his way home every day. It must have served him well, because Sam fought his way to the top of a big, tough union. And he was doing a great job for them getting their retirement plan completed.

We got along so well in our work that he eventually became the co-chairman of the Labor Management Council in Kansas

City. That was also when I got to know Bill Dunn, who was on the management side and something the opposite of Sam.

As time went on, Sam began to come around. He was located in a big union building at 63rd and Holmes. I would go out there and visit with him in his offices. And slowly the man started dressing up to the job. I felt proud of the transformation over the course of the three years I worked with him.

And since he was labor, he was a big Democrat, heavy into politics. He had pictures of some Republicans, like Nixon and Reagan, on the side of his building. They were caricatures with long noses like Pinocchio. About this same time I was also on the board of the Convention and Visitors Bureau, which I have been for nearly 40 years. One day Mayor Richard Berkley came to me to talk to Sam about taking them down. We were trying to get the Republican National Convention at the time, and Mayor Berkley was worried someone from the committee would see them.

"Sam, you and I are good Democrats and buddies," I told him. "Will you do me a big favor? I know you hate those guys, but would you do something about the caricatures on the side of your building?"

"For you, I'll do it," he told me.

So he got big tarps and put them on the side of the building and covered the faces. The Republicans never came to town for their convention, and Sam took the tarps down for everyone to see what he thought of the Republicans again.

Sam got embroiled in some serious stuff, too. One year there was construction going on at a downtown building. There was some kind of crane accident and a worker was killed. OSHA came in and investigated. Later it was concluded that it was the operator's fault. The operator, of course, was one of Sam's men. The day it happened Sam went down to the building and re-created the whole accident with Tinker Toys. It was unbelievable when he presented the model during the trial. Eventually, because of the Tinker Toys, the jury agreed that Sam was right.

Later, though, Sam was indicted for something else. The judge in Kansas City found him innocent. But some always felt that Sam's involvement with the union and the Democrats was the reason he had been indicted since the Republicans were in power at the time. The verdict was appealed, and eventually he was found guilty by another judge, who gave him probation and a $50 fine!

But Sam was such a force and so popular in Kansas City because of his charity work. Despite what had happened he was named the head of the United Way Drive.

A life-long Democrat, I have always been proud of my association with Sam and labor. I have worked hard on labor's behalf. In 1989, thanks in large measure to Sam, I was named UNICO's Man of the Year.

"His commitment is inspiring and his approach to problem solving is both practical and compassionate," Sam wrote in the program. "My good friend, Bill Grigsby, is a leader.

"He understands the feelings and emotions of others. His charisma makes people feel valued and strengthened through the magic of communication, thoughtful, persuasive communication. Those of you who know Bill have seen and felt the deep patriotism, the sense of purpose and the dedication he brings to every effort.

"Bill Grigsby is just a 'regular guy,' but he's no ordinary man."

To this day, Sam and I remain good friends, although I do not see him as much as I would like.

I joined the Mark Twain Bank team in 1980. I enjoyed Mark Twain because the people were like me. We all worked well together; them as bankers and me as their spokesman. It went well. On the weekends I was doing the Chiefs and during the week the banking biz, putting in probably 30 hours a week. I saw a lot of fine men and women develop and grow up in that system who are today running banks throughout Kansas City.

It was in 1999 when Mercantile bought the organization. I went with the deal. But when I made the transition to the seventh floor of the Mercantile Towers I saw a management team that did not smile a lot. Nobody smiled.

That atmosphere, though, only motivated me. I wanted to change the attitude. And I am happy to say that in about three months I had everybody smiling, laughing and generally feeling good about life on the seventh floor. With that mission accomplished, I then took it upon myself to go down into the lobby at noon hour where I would find a lot of folks standing in line disgruntled. I started having fun, telling them jokes and Chiefs stories. It was a great time and things worked out well.

Then First Star came in and bought Mercantile. After that, U.S. Bank came and brought people who were simply not my style. They were what I would call big-city bankers. But Kansas City to me is not Big City Bank. The reason Mark Twain had done so well is that it had a small, friendly hometown feel to its management. During the time I was there, the bank was heavy into real estate loans, which helped the town grow.

Look at Crosby Kemper at UMB. He is not a big-city guy. He is a good guy. He fits in with the community. It is the people like him who have made Kansas City a strong town.

I was associated with banking for nearly 25 years. I know people do not associate me with that industry. That's because I was not a real banker. Those guys would not have let me loan 30 cents to anyone. I think I am smart enough to have been a banker, but my role was to let those other guys run the banking and let me be the up-front good guy.

I have always tried to contribute. It has always been my intent to give something, whether it to be my family, friends or community. Anytime you are in the public venue you are called upon, and it's important that you respond positively. And I think I do a pretty good job of helping people raise money. It is just part of my "give-back philosophy." I am no saint, but I do feel I have been blessed all my life, even when we were poor. I feel I have to give that blessing back in some way, because I have been fortunate in good health and my children have been fortunate in good health.

"Bill should have been an evangelist, because life is always beautiful in his world," said Mickey Finn, a crony of mine in the Northland who owns a public relations firm. "He puts more miles on his car each year attending speaking events, charities and auctions than does a highway patrolman. He can walk into a room knowing no one and walk out knowing everybody."

My favorite lesson in living came while visiting a nursing home. I was chatting with a vivacious lady who was 104 years young and whose mind was still very active. I asked her, "To what do you attribute your long and useful life?"

She replied, "I give love. I get love!"

Another time I was visiting a nursing home and met this beautiful lady. I figure everybody knows who I am in Kansas City. So I said to her, "Ma'am do you know who I am?" She replied, "No, but if you go back to the front desk, they can probably tell you."

I know I'm seen as the ultimate jokester, but my really close friends sometimes see a different persona.

"He's misunderstood to some degree," my longtime friend, Preston Williams, will tell you. "He's a lot softer guy that what people think. He's not exactly an 'easy touch', but he's a softer human being. I know he likes to give the impression he's brisk with witticisms. But he's really so much softer and warmer than the stand-up comedian that he portrays."

Thanks, Preston.

I love my community and have received an enormous amount of love back from my community. There is a Greek proverb that says that the heart that loves is always young.

Fran and I keep a file of notes and letters I get after I have spoken or been involved with various organizations in both the Midwest and around the country. It does my heart good to browse through these from time to time.

The Lions Club, the Leukemia Society, Fund for Rural Education and Development, AFL-CIO, Epilepsy Foundation, Kansas City Crime Commission, United Cerebral Palsy, Missouri State Troopers Association, Ladies of Charity, Special Olympics, Boy Scouts, Girl Scouts, American Lung Association, March of Dimes, Department of Veterans Affairs, Boys and Girls Clubs, Alliance for Nonviolent Programming, Women Helping Women, Department of Justice.

Head Injury Association, American Diabetes Association, National Kidney Foundation, United Way, Our Lady of Mercy Home, Cystic Fibrosis Foundation, Little Sisters of the Poor, American Cancer Society…

The list goes on.

I am extremely proud of my involvement with these kinds of groups that do so much good in our world. Actually, this is only a small sampling of the many organizations I will go out of my way to help in any way possible.

"The special love and concern that you have for the NAIA was never more evident than during the March 14 Civic Appreciation Luncheon…" Harry Fritz, executive director, wrote me once.

Over the last couple of decades, I have probably been involved with 50 major charities by raising money or giving time and effort. I have lent my name to golf tournaments, roasts and other kinds of celebrity events.

I enjoy golf a great deal but love making charity golf tournaments a success. "Your sparkling personality helped to make this year's tournament the most successful ever," wrote Karen Long, executive director for the Cystic Fibrosis Foundation.

Personality, pooh. Sometimes it simply takes rolling up your sleeves and working hard to pull off a successful outing for those in need. I have always dedicated myself to the so-called mercedarian missionaries.

"You were the one who instigated this lovely affair and we want you to know how much we appreciate your efforts…you lightened many people's lives." Signed, Sister Mary Margaret Sneddon of Our Lady of Mercy Home.

Because of my background and my brother Jimmy's sacrifice, I especially have a soft spot for men and women of the military. They are frequently taken away from home and there is uncertainty whether they will make it home.

I am currently highly involved at Whiteman Air Force Base near Knob Noster, Missouri. Brigadier General Leroy Barnidge, the commander of the 509th bomb wing, asked me to speak at the annual Air Force dinner. I did, and he and I developed a friendship. I got to know a lot of the people on the line over there, and I have even gotten to fly the Stealth bomber simulator.

What I have tried to do is bring the community closer together with the service and the base there. It is important for the people in the KC area to know what is going on at Whiteman Air Force Base. Out of Whiteman flies the greatest air power in the world. That power, the stealth bomber, has changed the face of combat globally.

But it is not just the current servicemen whom I care deeply about. We should never forget about the sacrifice of the many veterans of this country. I have always kept that in mind and responded whenever a veterans group called.

"Once again, thank you," began the letter from the Department of Veterans Affairs. "You have established a long and proud tradition of honoring the heroes of our Armed Forces. I don't know how we could stage our activities without you."

Emotional support is crucial, but so too is raising bucks.

"As an auctioneer, you're the best!" wrote the Boys and Girls Clubs of Greater Kansas City. "I had hoped for $3,000 and you took us over $11,000. Wow! You're amazing."

"The tournament was a great success…thanks to your sweet, generous heart, the Kidney Foundation has gotten a start on what will be our biggest fund raiser."

I have been involved in Special Olympics about as long as they have been in existence. I have been on their board, been honored by them and raised money for them. I really enjoy those kids and the families who spend a lot of time with that organization.

"At this time it looks as though we will raise between $19,000 and $23,000 for the Special Olympics program…may God Bless You!"

Like I have been saying throughout these pages, I HAVE been blessed. There is great reward in helping others.

"Thanks so much for being the MC at the 14th annual Wheel Chair Games closing banquet…your wit, charm and enthusiasm helped make what is usually a dull, boring evening one of fun and excitement."

And sometimes the reward might be something more tangible. Not that I needed this kind of favor.

"On behalf of the Bluejacket PTA...thank you for sharing your time and wisdom with our sixth graders."

Fran and many of my friends might say that my wisdom does not extend past the sixth-grade level!

The truth is I have trouble saying no to anybody. At least that is what Fran will tell you. If I can squeeze it in, I don't say no. I have an ongoing list of people who have helped me, and if I don't give back, what am I doing on this earth?

Back to business, my first game back from the heart attack.

Skidmore put me in business. Merle Harmon helped me in many, many ways. Lamar...Stram...Dawson...Petersen.

The great thing is that the more I became known throughout my life, the more I could help people. But do not misunderstand, I have not gotten so involved because I needed exposure. I did it because somebody had to do it. I very seldom called upon people like Lenny Dawson, Lamar Hunt or Hank, because I was uncomfortable, knowing that they were so busy.

And it is just downright fun to get letters from famous and important people.

"Bill...thanks so much...I enjoyed seeing you once again and appreciate all that you do for college football. Your friend, Tom (Osborne, Nebraska football coach)."

"Bill...in a day when college athletics are subject to daily "bashing," it is rewarding to find those who understand and appreciate the values of amateur sports. Warm regards, Bill (Snyder, Kansas State football coach)."

"Bill and Fran...many thanks for including us. Sincerely, Carl (Peterson, Chiefs President).

Sometimes the words were not so nice.

"Mr. Grigsby," the card began.

"We have just heard on the radio that you have been broadcasting about the Chiefs since 1963. Now that is just wonderful to many people who have nothing more worthwhile to do all day.

"We agree that you have several sound citizens on the Chiefs payroll who earn their money and are a help in building the KC community. But most of the players are just overgrown bums that the community would be better off without.

"The civilized communities of the world have eliminated bullfights and it would be fine if they would eliminate such so-called professional fights as your Chiefs perform. It would be fine if our legislators would eliminate so-called professional football and you too, if that would be necessary. (Signed) Kansas City Business Owners"

Thank goodness the sentiment has changed since I received that on February 3, 1970.

Thank you to the famous and not so famous who have bothered to write or call with their thanks for whatever small way I have been able to help in your life. One of the most touching notes I have ever received came just before Christmas 1996 after I had dedicated our Chiefs broadcast to a young man by the name of Jake Jasperson. It still touches me greatly every year during the holidays.

"Dear Mr. Grigsby,

"Just a note to thank you for dedicating the game to my dear patient. He was so thrilled! He is a young man with a very aggressive lymphoblastic lymphoma. He is 19 years old. I gave him chemo 3 1/2 years ago and he went into remission.

"Six months ago his disease recurred. Currently, he's very end stage. I doubt if he will live until Christmas. But he is such an inspiration to all who know him.

"I'm a certified oncology nurse and again, I thank you for being so kind in dedicating the game to him!

"Angels are everywhere!

"Sincerely, Dixie Wright, RNN."

God put us all on this earth for a purpose. Part of my purpose is to help and be compassionate of others. Some might question my sincerity, I realize that. But I don't care what those people think. There are people who have their own agenda, but I try not to make them a part of mine. It suits me to try to do things quietly, but sometimes that is hard to do.

In the end, my greatest talent has not been in front of a microphone, a TV camera, or dais. If I have had a true calling it has been my energy and desire to bring others together in some sort of positive way. I have been fortunate to be able to do that.

At my current age, I ponder everything that I have seen. What a magnificent time to have lived. To be born when I was and to be here today to see such progress in so many areas. To go through the Depression and now for our society to enjoy such prosperity. To go through three wars. To be a part of the fun of the National Football League. To have satisfied a life-long dream of broadcasting Major League sports and seeing it grow and grow.

To be a part of it all has been wonderful. Happiness and harmony comes by caring about others and impacting their lives.

In the morning when I get up, I take vitamins. Before dinner, vodka. My doctor tells me as long as I don't ever reverse it, everything will be beautiful.

For Grigs…its been a beauuutiful life.